DOOR

~*~ OF ~*~

HOPE

Revised and Updated

JAN FRANK

THOMAS NELSON PUBLISHERS
OCM3/24/3458
Nashville

Published in Nashville, Tennessee, by Thomas Nelson, Inc.

Library of Congress Cataloging-in-Publication Data

Frank, Jan.
   Door of hope : recognizing and resolving the pains of your past / Jan Frank. — Rev. & updated.
      p. cm.
   Includes bibliographical references and index.
   ISBN-10 0-7852-7966-0
   ISBN-13 978-0-7852-7966-2
   1. Abused women—Pastoral counseling of. 2. Incest victims—Pastoral counseling of. 3. Adult child abuse victims—Pastoral counseling of. 4. Christian life—1960- 5. Frank, Jan. I. Title.
BV4445.5.F73   1995
248.8'6—dc20   94-24343
                                                                              CIP

Printed in the United States of America
13 14 15 16 QG 25 24 23 22

This book is dedicated to my dear husband, Don, whose patience, support and love sustained me during the healing process detailed in this book. It was through his encouragement, self-sacrifice and commitment to the Lord's purpose in our lives that this book was completed.

And to our little girls, Heather and Kellie, whom the Lord continually uses to teach me about His Father's heart of love.

CONTENTS

Several years ago at a seminar in Tulsa, the noted therapist Karl Menninger made this statement: "In the USA today, incest is becoming about as commonplace as shoplifting." At the time I was startled and thought he might be exaggerating. Unfortunately, the rapidly-rising statistics and my own counseling experience confirm how accurate he was.

Only in recent years has the church acknowledged the fact that incest is prevalent within the Christian community. How well I remember helping a young co-ed from a conservative Christian family find healing from her devastating memories of incest. When she finally reminded her mother of how she had tried as a teenager to tell her, the mother broke down and confessed that, because she, too, had been a victim, she didn't know what to do. Later, when they both shared this with an elderly grandmother, she wept and confessed to the same experience. The greatest tragedy was that, when both mother and daughter had gone to their pastors for help, they were commanded not to tell anyone because "it would destroy the church!"

We owe Jan Frank a debt of gratitude, for with the publication of this book, she was one of the first to bring the problem to the attention of Christians. Her honesty and understanding about the hurt and humiliation of what she experienced gives other victims the courage necessary to face the truth, and the hope necessary to believe healing is possible. Her clearly outlined steps then provide practical suggestions for the painful process of recovery.

I have loaned her book out many times as a form of bibliotherapy for such women, and watched it help bring about transformation and wholeness in their lives. I also recommend it to pastors and counselors. They will find this new edition of her book, with the addendum of answers to the most frequently asked questions, more valuable than ever.

David A. Seamands,
Healing for Damaged Emotions

ACKNOWLEDGEMENTS

Special thanks to the many anonymous victims whose lives are represented in this book.

Thanks also to:

Lauren Briggs, who spent endless hours at her computer deciphering my handwriting and translating it into a readable manuscript.

Darlene Grierson, my sister-in-law, whose encouragement gave me confidence and whose knowledge of grammar and punctuation added clarity to the manuscript.

Pam Houston and Dr. Laurel Basbas, whose prayer support and faithfulness to God's call in their lives continue to encourage and minister healing to me.

Amy Clark, for her creativity in designing the cover, and all those at Thomas Nelson who respected my desire to maintain the *Door of Hope* photograph, taken by my friend, Chuck Noon, so many years ago.

Our devoted prayer group: Don, Mary, Lynn, Dave, Chris, and Mae, for faithfully praying for me during this project.

My dearest friends, Ginny and Patsy, whose love and friendship enrich my life and draw me close to my Savior.

Dotty Stephenson, who has been a spiritual mother to me and a devoted intercessor on my behalf.

My husband, Don, who has been God's choicest vessel in teaching me about the love of my heavenly Father.

The God of all comfort, whose love and mercy continue to bring healing to the heart of this child.

The greatest joy I receive is knowing many, who through reading this book, have been encouraged to pursue God's healing and wholeness in their lives. Over the years I have learned that this journey is really not about recovery from sexual abuse—it is about knowing God. I firmly believe that God wants to remove any obstacles in our lives that prevent us from knowing who we are in Him, and who He truly is. I rejoice when I hear of one person whose relationship with God has been transformed, a captive who's been set free from the bondage of the past, a prisoner liberated from the distortions planted by the enemy of our souls.

When I began praying about doing a revised version of the book, it seemed as though I kept hitting a roadblock. I did not have a peace about making major changes in the body of the manuscript. The more I prayed, the more I sensed the Lord leading me to compose an addendum of commonly asked questions and their answers. So many readers over the years have written me letters of encouragement, shared their painful histories, and asked numerous questions that have plagued their hearts.

The addendum reflects many of the questions I am commonly asked. It is important to note that, since these questions and answers can only provide general information, it may be necessary for you to obtain counsel from someone with whom you can share more personally.

Also, in the addendum I've attempted to provide an update

of the continued healing God has done in my own life since the book was first published.

Thirteen years ago, at age twenty-seven, I had to face depression, anger, migraine headaches, a critical attitude, low self-esteem, and the feelings of distance from God that characterized my life. Now, at age forty, I look back and am in awe as I reflect upon God's immeasurable grace in my life. Now, instead of despair, I live with joy, peace, healing, intimacy with God, freedom, and redemption. He truly has restored to me the years the locusts had eaten. I can truly say that, if I had the power to change the events of my life, I would not—

For it has been, through the PAIN that I've known His PEACE, through the HEARTACHE I've embraced His HEALING, and through the VALLEY I've discovered His VICTORY.

O the deep, deep love of Jesus!

Jan Frank, July 1994

CHAPTER 1

Healing Emotional Wounds

WHEN WORDS FAIL, TEARS FLOW.
— *Chuck Swindoll*

One crisp evening, I was at a women's retreat sharing my FREE TO CARE recovery steps for the healing of emotional wounds when I noticed Joanne sobbing quietly in the last row of the rustic meeting room. Joanne, a small vivacious woman in her thirties, related well to the other women. She had appeared trouble free, yet now she was weeping in the arms of a friend.

Several minutes after speaking I was able to work my way back to Joanne. I reached out and put my arms around her as she choked out these words, "I've never let myself cry since I lost my little boy six years ago. He was only ten months old when he died. After all these years I'm still angry at God."

Joanne gazed into my eyes and said, "When you spoke tonight, Jan, I realized I'd never fully faced Timmy's death. I've never let myself grieve completely. Everyone told me I should count my blessings since I still had two healthy children. Two months after Timmy's death, my friends said it was time to cheer up and get on with my life."

Like many of us, Joanne decided to put on a mask to cover the intensity of her pain.

When Beth, a strikingly beautiful pastor's wife, approached me for counseling at a women's brunch, I wondered what could be wrong. As we sat on a step beneath the platform her story unfolded. She was a victim of molestation as a child and had an abortion as a teenager. Only recently she had learned her husband was having an affair with one of her friends. Tears welled up in Beth's eyes as she asked, "What do I do? I'm so hurt. My husband has admitted his affair. He's told me we have to forget about it and go on for the sake of his ministry." Beth trembled slightly, then added, "He's refused to answer any of my questions because he says forgiveness means not being concerned about the details. I don't feel like I have anyone to talk to and I can't get over some of the feelings I'm having. Jan, what you said today made sense. I know I need to go through this healing process if I am going to be free."

Like many of us, Beth assumed forgiveness means covering the pain and pretending it doesn't exist.

Last week my phone rang while I was preparing dinner. "Jan?" came the troubled voice on the other end. "This is Charlotte. I'm going to kill myself if I don't get some answers."

I whispered a quick prayer for guidance and asked, "Charlotte, what happened?"

"I don't know what to think anymore," she answered. "I went to my pastor for counseling today. His first question to me was, 'Why haven't you been in church?' I explained to him that I'm having trouble relating to God because of my past, but that I'm currently in therapy trying to work things out. He cut me off, saying, 'You don't need therapy. Just start being obedient and get your life right with God.'"

As I listened to Charlotte, her voice became more desperate. "Jan, when I tried to explain to my pastor that being molested as a child had taken a toll on my life and marriage, he immediately corrected me. He said the problem was my rebelliousness and that I just needed to be submissive to my

2

abusive ex-husband and to quit going to therapy for the answers that only God could give."

Charlotte paused then blurted, "Jan, I was so shook up after the session, I called a friend from church who had been my confidante in the past. When I told her what the pastor said, she fully supported him. She added, 'If you don't get your life in shape, Charlotte, God told me He's going to take away your little girl and your house and you'll live alone the rest of your life.' She ended by saying, 'God is your only hope, so you'd better straighten up.'"

Sobbing, she continued, "Jan, if that's *really* who God is, then I might as well kill myself."

Like many of us, Charlotte's view of God had been distorted by her experiences in life.

My own parents divorced when I was five years old. When I was eight, Mother remarried. My stepfather was a Christian man who attended church regularly. At the age of ten I went forward in an evening church service and asked Christ into my life as my personal Savior. Three weeks later my stepfather molested me.

Incest! The word is ugly. The act is devastating.

Years passed. I married a wonderful Christian man and two years into our marriage our first little girl was born. In the days that followed, the harder I tried to care for our vulnerable, colicky baby, the more desperate and out-of-control I became. That desperation triggered the memory of the helplessness that I felt as a ten-year-old. My past began to haunt me. Migraine headaches and nightmares became frequent. I struggled with intense, explosive anger. I was depressed, critical with my husband and I felt undeserving of God's love. I had prayed for years that God would help me forgive my stepfather so that I could go on with my life. I thought that was all there was to it. But I was wrong.

The Holy Spirit showed me that I needed to go through a healing process. The rest of this book details that ten-step process.

Throughout the book I have attempted to balance real-life experiences, biblical principles and current factual literature. I have focused on the incest victim, not only because of my personal experience, but because I am convinced after counseling thousands of persons that sexual victimization in childhood is pandemic. "Statistics indicate that thirty-four million women in the United States are victims of child sexual abuse. It is estimated that a child is molested every two minutes."[1] A recent *Los Angeles Times* poll showed that nearly one out of every four people in the United States has been molested as a child; and that for every victim known, nine are hidden.[2]

As I've shared my ten-step FREE TO CARE recovery plan nationwide, I've found that it applies to any emotional wound we may have suffered. This is not a simplistic plan that can be carried out in a matter of weeks. Nor is it a magical formula that can be instantly and impulsively undertaken, but rather, it is a pathway toward the resolution of past hurts. Those who utilize these steps should be committed to prayer and to allowing the Holy Spirit to provide direction and wisdom. These steps give direction and they put us in a position to be healed, but *the Holy Spirit completes the work*. The Scripture says the Holy Spirit's work in our lives is to lead us into all truth. Psalm 51:6 says: "Behold, thou desirest truth in the inward parts: and in the hidden part thou shalt make me to know wisdom."

I believe emotional recovery occurs over a period of time. It's not that the Lord doesn't have the ability to heal us instantly. He does. I have found, however, that He often uses a process of time for our instruction and renewing. It is similar to our coming to know Christ. Although we are instantly new

4

creatures in Him, we are in the process of being "conformed to the image of his Son" (Rom. 8:29) throughout our lives.

The ten steps to recovery helped Joanne face the loss of her baby boy and freed her to grieve. These steps showed Beth that she needed to be honest about her feelings regarding her husband's unfaithfulness. She needed to work through her pain in order to be free. The FREE TO CARE steps have encouraged Charlotte to go on living. Today her relationship with God is free from scars and distortions.

I, too, am free today. I am no longer held captive by the pain of my past. The Lord has taken the desolation of my life and caused it to bear fruit. He is the *only* one who can do that.

Many of you may be asking, "Why is it necessary for us to look into our past? Shouldn't we just forget those things and go on with life?

If we could genuinely forget, there would be no need to look back. But for many of us the pain of our past still creeps into our daily lives. Pain not adequately dealt with or worked through warps our ability to live in the freedom God has for us in Christ.

I have shared many personal experiences of my own healing in hopes that those who are still bound by their past will be encouraged to pursue recovery. My burden for those who are hurting is summed up in the beautiful promise in Isaiah 58:12(KJV): "And they that shall be of thee shall build the old waste places: thou shalt *raise up* the foundations of many generations; and thou shalt be called, The *repairer* of the breach, The *restorer* of paths to dwell in" (italics mine).

This verse helped me understand the needs I had had and the needs of others who are hurting. It identifies specific goals to use when trying to help them. First, we should *raise* the wounded up. Second, we need to help them *repair* their broken and shattered lives. Third, we need to *restore* them to a healthy path. As I looked at these words in the Hebrew, I was fascinated by the depth of their meaning.

Raise Up

The Hebrew word pronounced *koom* means "to help to lift up, establish, strengthen, confirm, or authenticate." How many of us are raising up the ones who are hurting? Too many times Christians condemn others or hold them down by saying, "A spiritual Christian should not feel angry." We respond to the wounded with shock and rejection when they need to be strengthened and re-established in their relationship with God. Too often, we fail to understand that the hurts of their past are blocking a vital fellowship with God. Their wounds must be dealt with in order for them to be *raised up*!

Repair

The Hebrew word for repair is pronounced *gawder*, and is a descriptive word meaning "to walk in or around, to close up, hedge or enclose." I immediately think of the emotionally wounded who need to sense a hedge about them and to be sheltered or nurtured within a protective environment. One of the first things we are advised to do to treat a wound is to clean it thoroughly and then cover it with a protective cloth to ward off infection.

What an example for emotional wounds! Hurts must be cleansed and provided with a protective, supportive environment where they can begin to heal. Christians can provide that kind of environment for those who are hurting, for the thousands who need to be *repaired*!

Restore

The final step is the Hebrew word pronounced *shoob*. It means "to rescue, recover, retrieve, to bring back home again or cause to make to return." Many who have been hurt are in need of restoration. They need to be brought home again, but many times their wounds keep them bound, immobilized. Restoration means to bring them to the one who is able to restore them and heal them from the inside out. The wounded need to be *restored*!

As you read the rest of this book, I encourage you to consider your needs carefully and make yourself available to the Holy Spirit for His restorative work. Daniel 2:22 says: "He reveals the deep and secret things; He knows what is in the darkness and the light dwells with Him!" (Amplified Version). Ask for His enlightenment to penetrate the dark areas of your hurt. It is only through this exposure that you can truly begin to face what has happened in your past and move on through the healing process.

Will you allow the Holy Spirit to begin to expose those troubled areas in your life? Will you allow His light to heal those hurts? Will you let Him set you free?

CHAPTER 2

Step I.

Face the Problem

T he first step to recovery is to face the problem—the infected wound that hasn't healed.

Susan is forty-two years old. She is married and has two teenage children. Her husband is in Christian work and is dedicated to his family. They have been getting marriage counseling off and on for several years. Susan shares that the focal point of their problems seems to be their sexual relationship. Her husband is growing weary because counseling has done little to help Susan get over her hang-ups.

Thirty-two-year-old Carla has been divorced three times. Carla confesses that she always seems to attract men who end up abusing her emotionally or physically. She has determined to get her life in order, but repeatedly finds herself involved in poor relationships.

Diane, twenty-nine and single, is grossly overweight. She is depressed and has tried every diet on the market. She is contemplating having her jaws wired but realizes she really doesn't want to control her eating habits.

Mary, a devoted mother and wife, spends time reading her Bible and praying, but she feels God isn't listening. Mary has counseled with her pastor but is still struggling in her Christian walk.

What, if anything, do these women have in common? If

they come to you for counseling, what would you tell them? Do you identify with any of their struggles?

These women are real people who came to me with their problems. You may know others like them. You may even be one of them. What you do not know is that each of these women is a victim of incest. Incest is defined as any sexual contact between people who are, or perceive themselves to be, related. Sexual abuse occurs outside the family constellation. These women are manifesting the symptoms that plague many sexual abuse victims. But, like most victims, they are unaware that their present problem has anything to do with their past, that it is the result of a deeper, more complex condition known as the "root problem."

The Root-Bound Plant

Picture a lovely green philodendron, a houseplant which must be repotted periodically to prevent its becoming rootbound. Since this condition exists below the surface, a rootbound plant can be in that state for quite some time before anyone notices anything wrong. After a while, however, the plant's leaves turn brown, the soil hardens, and the plant begins to smell rotten. The leaves eventually drop off and the once rich green plant shows signs of a problem. Many well-intentioned plant lovers might tell you, "Oh, just keep watering your philodendron. Give it some sun, change its location, talk to it, pray for it or read it some Bible verses. It will come back to life in no time and the symptoms will disappear."

The well-informed gardener, however, will tell you something different. He will tell you it needs to be in a larger pot, but he will caution against just digging it up. Further steps—examining the plant, breaking apart its roots and giving it new soil—are essential in the process of restoring the plant. This process is a "painful" experience for a plant and often it may temporarily go into "shock." However, the end result, after some time of nurturing and caring, will be a healthy, thriving green philodendron that is lovelier than ever before. Should you elect to ignore the plant's earlier condition, it will eventually die.

If you are a sexual abuse victim, you are much like the root-bound plant. You may go on for years without any visible symptoms, but eventually surface problems will appear. Often these are visible as depression, anger, marital difficulties, migraines, anxiety, eating disorders, or feeling distant from God. The tendency of well-meaning Christians is to treat the surface symptoms, but that is like trimming up the root-bound plant to make it attractive on the outside. This fails to deal with the real problem. In the meantime, the surface symptoms will reappear, often with greater seriousness than before. In his book *Healing of Memories*, David Seamands writes, "When painful memories have not been faced, healed and integrated into life, they often break through defenses and interfere with normal living."[1]

If you are a victim, it may be necessary for you to dig up the past events and, along with a qualified therapist or support person(s), begin to examine the past, dissect it, break it apart, and carefully work through what has happened. This is what I call facing the problem. Just as with the plant, it is often a painful process. In time, with the support and caring of others, you will begin to show new signs of life. You'll be free from the root-bound condition that has held you captive for years and you can begin to experience a fuller, healthier life.

Three Types of Victims

In working with victims, I have found them to be in three basic categories: repressed, suppressed and oppressed.

1. *The Repressed Victim.* First, there is the woman who is unaware that anything of an incestuous/abusive nature ever happened. She has blocked the memory due to the intense trauma she experienced as a child. She often exhibits the same symptoms as women who have not blocked the memory.

Usually she will be depressed; often, she is suicidal. Many times she is physically racked with inexplicable pain. There is little hope for this type of victim until she becomes aware of the underlying causes of her depression and other symptoms.

While speaking at a church in central California, I became acquainted with Kay. Kay suffered from severe depression, lapses of memory from childhood, and physical ailments which seemed to have no known origin. I encouraged her to seek counseling to help her explore the depression and the years that were absent from her memory. She sought counseling at my suggestion. Through intense therapy she discovered she had, indeed, blocked the memories of a series of incestuous acts instigated by her father as early as when she was three. Through therapy and the support of other victims, she is working through the crisis and has made a great deal of progress.

2. *The Suppressed Victim.* The second type of victim is aware of an incident or incidents in her life, but has suppressed the memory, feeling it has little relevance to her today. She may have sexual problems in her marriage, low self-esteem and an inability to establish close relationships. The support group setting and/or therapy can help her work through many of her difficulties in the present which stem from her past.

I met Barb, one of these victims, in a Bible study I was teaching. Barb exhibited many of the symptoms common to victims. After sharing my story one day, she confided that she had been touched by her brother when she was young. She said she'd nearly forgotten it and that "it wasn't a big deal anyway." It took Barb a year to realize that the incidents of her past were playing a significant role in her relationships today, especially with her husband. Barb joined a support group and is finding she is not alone.

3. *The Oppressed Victim.* The third category is a victim who remembers and identifies the trauma of the past, but who thinks she has resolved it. I was this type of victim. I had always

been aware of the incest and knew it had hurt me deeply. But for nearly twenty years I thought I had resolved it. Since I was aware and had asked the Lord to help me forgive my stepfather, I thought it had all been taken care of, yet I lacked victory in my spiritual walk. There was oppression in my spirit. I, too, experienced most of the common symptoms of victims but did not recognize them. I was convinced that my mood swings, criticalness of my husband, and anger with my toddler were just part of the normal everyday stresses a woman experiences. Through counseling with friends and listening to the host on a Christian radio show, I began to realize that my problem was deeper. I sought individual therapy with a counselor who specialized in the area of incest. There were issues I needed to address and work through, step by step.

When I began to share the detailed steps that were necessary for me, other women began to be helped and lives began to be changed. Recovery is possible. It often takes time, but facing the problem is the start.

How Is Your Root System?
To face the problem, you must take an honest look at your life. It is what the Scriptures call "examining yourself." The intent is not to degrade or condemn, but to evaluate yourself in truth. As I did this, I realized I could no longer pretend. I had presented a false image of confidence, peacefulness and spirituality in the presence of others but inside I was insecure, angry and distant from God. If you are a person whose internal state significantly differs from the external, you may be covering up some wounds.

No matter what type of deep hurt you've experienced, resolution can come only when you're willing to face the problem. That includes facing what has happened and looking honestly at any symptoms that have resulted. Until we are willing to do this, the Holy Spirit is limited in accomplishing the deep work of healing.

Symptoms of the Root-Bound Condition

Most victims of abuse experience common symptoms. We will look at nine of them in detail: depression, anger, fear/anxiety, guilt/shame, difficulty establishing relationships, repeated victimization, shut-off/over-controlling of emotions, sexual problems in marriage, and poor self-image/low self-esteem. These generalized symptoms provide a basis for which further exploration is indicated. But remember, many of these symptoms are typical experiences in life. It is when these symptoms persist and occur in combination that we must consider that some type of victimization or emotional injury *may* have taken place.

1. *Depression.* If you are a victim, you may experience depression that can range from a periodic mild depression to a severe one lasting for months.

Darla, a lovely dedicated Christian in my first support group, found herself despondent and contemplating suicide. Fortunately, she admitted herself to a Christian psychiatric hospital where, for the first time, she became aware of an incestuous event perpetrated by her father. By confronting her depression, she was able to work through the trauma of her past and is currently ministering to others who are hurting.

For some victims, depression has been a way of life. I had always considered myself to be moody. During the early years of our marriage, I asked my husband, Don, why he didn't spend more time talking with me and sharing his feelings. "Frankly," he said, "I have had to be so careful about what I said to you, it just wasn't worth it." I would often plunge into the depths of despair over one of his innocent, insignificant comments. Don found it safer to be silent.

The depression felt by victims may come and go, and can be triggered by almost anything: an article in a newspaper, a phone conversation, the holiday season, or an innocuous comment made by a friend. Where does it come from?

Depression is a state of feeling helpless. If you were victimized as a child, you probably experienced a feeling of being helplessly trapped. You were unable to express your anger and confusion over being violated. You carried that anger within, and depression became a coping mechanism. Victims don't like being held captive by their emotions, but they can't change on their own. A woman in Texas wrote, "I feel I don't know myself or what I can do in this life. I get so depressed that I feel like I can't even call out to God for help." Until victims deal with the root problem, change may never occur. Even then, the patterns they have developed take time to change.

Are you struggling with depression in your life? You need to face it. Call it what it is and find the root cause in order to be free.

2. *Anger.* The anger that victims experience is usually misdirected. Many deny it even exists. Carol, who was in a Bible study I led, talked about seeing her cousin during the holidays. As she related her family history and her relationship to this cousin, she blushed scarlet and her body tensed. She summed up by saying, "Of course, I don't hold anything against him anymore because I've forgiven him." I gently interjected that I sensed she was still angry with him for what he had done. Carol vehemently declared, "I am *not* angry with him. I've forgiven him." Others in the group pointed out that her body language indicated otherwise, but she emphatically insisted with a louder voice and a flushed face, "I am *not* angry. It's in the past and has been forgotten." It was obvious that Carol was not in touch with her anger.

In my own life, I began to exhibit outbursts of anger months before I was aware I had a problem in this area. I was angry with my boss when he overruled a decision I made. I was angry at a speeding driver. I was angry at a young boy who trespassed on our property. I was angry at my husband for pouring too much cereal for my daughter's breakfast. I was angry at my toddler for crying for "no good reason." In psychological terms, the anger was being displaced—directed at someone or something other than the true source.

Not until I went through therapy did I recognize the deep reservoir of anger I had stored for years. The source of the anger was in the whole incestuous relationship and was primarily directed toward my mother and stepfather. Because victims usually come from a family which suffers some type of dysfunction, the incest is only one expression of the breakdown in the family system. There were other incidents and circumstances in my family life that merited my anger; the incest, however, seemed to be the central issue.

If you are displacing your anger, realize it is often a carryover from your childhood. You were never allowed to express or even experience the emotions attached to the hurt. David Seamands states, "Time by itself does not and cannot heal those memories which are so painful that the experiences are as alive and painful ten or twenty years later as they were ten or twenty minutes after they were pushed out of consciousness."[2] The anger within starts like a simmering teakettle. By the time you reach adulthood, the kettle is boiling so vigorously that water and steam are escaping out of control. As you face the problem, you can begin to identify that anger and channel it toward its source.

3. *Fear/anxiety*. Are you a woman who fears the unknown and usually expects the worst? If your husband goes on a business trip are you convinced the plane will crash? If you see a documentary about earthquakes, do you feel certain your children will be trapped under the rubble? When you watch a news story on breast cancer are you sure you will end up needing a mastectomy? Victims often experience fears or anxieties in these ways. Phobias among victims are also quite

common. Many cannot go into elevators or any confining space. Others react to stressful situations by experiencing panic attacks or feeling extreme anxiety.

I would experience anxiety just prior to the holiday season. As the holidays approached I became more irritable and more on edge than usual. I screamed at my daughter, glared at my husband, and cried at the drop of a hat. One Thanksgiving day the drive to my parents' home was a struggle. Internally, my nerve endings were exposed. Even though I had prayed and asked the Lord to help me be loving, sensitive and kind, I felt a tightness in my body the entire day. I went away that day feeling like I had been through a battle zone. Nothing traumatic had happened. There were no confrontations or arguments. Nothing. Yet, I was an emotional wreck. Because this pattern developed every time I saw my stepfather, I finally realized there must be a connection. It was then that I decided to separate myself from him for an unspecified amount of time. This was one of the wisest decisions I made. It was a difficult one because it required me to make a choice on my own behalf. The year-long separation proved to be a significant factor in my recovery process.

The fear that is experienced by most victims might better be labeled intimidation. The woman who is faced with her aggressor finds herself reverting back to her role as a child. The sense of helplessness, rejection and fear all come to the surface and cause intense anxiety. Many victims have told me they still feel these emotions thirty years after the last incestuous contact. By helping victims develop their own self-image and by instructing them how to relate to their parents as adult daughters, they gain strength and are able to face their aggressors without fear.

4. *Guilt/shame.* The guilt felt by most victims is really *false* guilt. If you are a victim, you probably have assumed some responsibility for the incest and unknowingly have carried the

load of guilt for years. Many victims do not report feeling guilty as such, but feel ashamed or shameful for what has happened. For them this translates into their everyday lives as a feeling of being ridden with guilt about everything. For example, you and your family go on a picnic one Sunday afternoon after church. Before you know it, the storm clouds loom overhead and it begins raining. You immediately become depressed and withdrawn, and you apologize to your family—you obviously are at fault because you failed to read the weather report. Or your husband missed a dental appointment, and although you reminded him last week, you neglected to call his office the day of the appointment to remind him—so it's your fault. The circumstances are endless, and victims have a tendency to carry the guilt of their family and the whole world on their shoulders.

Guilt is often reflected in our relationship or lack of relationship with God. Are you a person who asks forgiveness continually and walks around for days paying penance? Do you have trouble accepting forgiveness? I could never understand how my husband could sin, ask God's forgiveness and go on with life. I would sin, plead for forgiveness for days, and feel weighed down by guilt. I was unable to accept God's forgiveness because I didn't feel I deserved it.

Some victims display a total reversal to this guilt-laden personality. They are controlling women who deny all responsibility and hold everyone accountable but themselves. Many have had several marriages and have little interest in delving into the past. They, too, are victims of guilt. They have shrouded their guilt in a defensiveness in order to survive. There is hope for them, but only after they are willing to face the problem and get to the source.

Where does the guilt come from? In many instances it has been placed there by the aggressor. You may have been told, "You look so cute in those little white shorts," or "You know your mother will be very angry with you if she finds out about this, so you'd better keep quiet." As an innocent child you were duped into thinking you were a "co-conspirator" or an accomplice in the incestuous act. For many, the guilt over their participation and the fear about the reprisals were so intense that the secret often remains intact for years. In a national survey conducted by the Los Angeles Times in July 1985, it was reported that prior to the survey, one in three victims had never told anyone about being molested.[3]

Is guilt or a feeling of shame a problem in your life? If so, it may be an indication of a deeper, hidden problem. Some victims will not even be able to recognize the fact that they feel guilt or shame. Others may be laden with it. The crucial point is recognizing that guilt has been falsely assumed. You must deal with the past in order to be free from the entanglement of guilt in the present.

5. *Difficulty establishing relationships.* Is this a problem for you? For most victims the difficulty in this area stems from a lack of trust. They are unable to allow people to get too close; at the same time, they have a deep need to be intimately associated with others. I received a phone call today from Karen, a single woman in our support group. "Did you hear what I did?" she asked.

"No." I answered.

"I took some pills this weekend," she responded. "The loneliness was just too much for me to handle. Jan, I feel so all alone." I spent the next few minutes reassuring her and trying to comfort her with loving affirmation.

It is not uncommon for victims to unknowingly sabotage the relationships they so desperately need. Both married and unmarried victims have difficulty in this area. If you are unmarried, you may have one or maybe two close female friends. You also may have a general sense of mistrust for females. You may have had numerous relationships with men or you may have had none. In either case, you may have an underlying suspicion toward men which may cause you to seek to have an upper hand or to withdraw and not get involved at all. If you are married, you may exhibit your mistrust by suspecting your husband of unfaithfulness. You may accuse him of wishing he had married someone else. Or you may be dissatisfied with him as a mate. Early in our marriage my husband, Don, wouldn't dare tell me that his secretary, Mary Lou, looked especially pretty at work that day. If he did, the wheels would turn in my head for days. I would interrogate Don about Mary Lou and *subtly* accuse him of believing that he would be happier with her. This mistrust ate away at our relationship. I knew where the source was and I told my husband how difficult it was for me to trust. I told him frankly one day, "Every man I ever had a relationship with has done me dirty. How am I to expect anything different from you?"

Don responded lovingly, but he earnestly challenged me, "Honey, you will get from me what you expect. If you expect complete faithfulness and trustworthiness, I will meet the challenge, but if you continue to mistrust and suspect me I will probably fall victim to your expectations."

I made a vow to him that day that I would go against all that my experience had taught me, and, by faith, I would trust him implicitly. It was hard to keep those mental wheels from turning at first, but the fruit of that decision has manifested itself in a greater love bond between us and a renewed sense of trust in our relationship.

Many times the victim's mistrust manifests itself in an inability to acquire and maintain an intimate relationship with God. Most victims at one time or another struggle with this issue. As they look back into the past and see where this comes from, it helps them to begin to change their patterns of relating. David Seamands comments, "Years of experience have taught me that regardless of how much correct doctrine Christians may know, until they have a picture and a felt sense that God is truly good and gracious, there can be no lasting spiritual victory in their lives."[4]

It is usually not difficult for the victim to see how the incest relates in this area. Someone she loved and trusted when she was a child inexcusably violated her physically and emotionally. The scars can be carried for life and are seen in an inability to secure and maintain intimacy with others. Do you have trouble trusting others? You can overcome your distrust and develop rich, meaningful relationships with others and with God, if you are willing to work through your past.

6. *Repeated victimization.* This symptom is so common among all types of victims that it is frightening. Many victims find themselves being victimized for years after the first incident. They may be victimized in a job, in a relationship, or in a marriage. Many women whom I have counseled see this as a pattern in their lives. One woman said, "It's as if I'm sending out vibes, or wearing a sign that says, 'Victimize Me.'" In a sense, they have unknowingly adopted this attitude, primarily about themselves.

I have spoken with countless women who share a similar story. One victim said, "When I began dating, I always seemed to be attracted to a guy who verbally abused me. I would stay in a terrible relationship for months, hoping I could change the guy into a sensitive, loving human being. Instead, I would end up totally defeated—an emotional basket case—from all the abuse I had taken. After several poor relationships, I finally got married only to discover I had married an alcoholic with a violent temper. I feel trapped, and yet, since I am a Christian, I feel bound to this marriage no matter what I must suffer."

For some, repeated victimization manifests itself in a job situation or a circumstance of life. You may be like Joan. She worked with a coworker who verbally and emotionally victimized her every day. Joan felt helpless and angry, but thought she had no alternatives.

This symptom has a ripple effect. A woman marries a man who victimizes her and her children. The victimized child, in turn, marries someone who victimizes her children—and the pattern goes on. Statistics indicate that 75 percent of the children who have been victimized within the home have mothers who were victims as children.[5] This is a demonstration of what the Scripture declares in Exodus 34:7: "Visiting the iniquity [sins] of the fathers upon the children and the children's children to the third and the fourth generation." One of the surest ways for a victim to break this pattern is to be aware of her own victimization and begin to work through her painful past.

The victim is drawn to people and/or circumstances she thinks she deserves. Victims are no different from anyone else when it comes to choosing the known versus the unknown. For most of us the known, no matter how painful or disgusting it may be, is far easier for us to choose than the unknown. This was demonstrated so clearly to me in my early career as juvenile hall counselor. I worked with abused and neglected children ranging in ages from birth to seventeen years. Many had been beaten, deprived, or sexually mistreated, and some had been burned with cigarette butts all over their bodies. When faced with the question of returning to their offender, usually a parent, or to an unknown foster home, most would opt for returning home. They knew what to expect there. As a victim, you have primarily known only one role from childhood: the victim role. As painful and devastating as it was, you know no alternative. You find yourself reverting to what you have "known" to be your lot in life. But, there is a door of hope for you. You can be helped to eradicate this symptom through rebuilding your self-image and through finding renewed relationships with God and with others.

7. *Shut-off/over-controlling of emotions.* Are you a person who has shut off your emotions? Don't stop reading, even if you answered no. Victims who suffer the shut-off of emotion are

often the most difficult to reach. They are women who appear to have everything under control. They seem confident to the point of being driven, independent to the point of being isolated, and controlled to the point of being insensitive. The reason they are difficult to reach is that they rarely recognize they have any problems. The more I work with victims, the more I come across these women. I, too, suffered from a need to be in control but I was totally unaware of it.

To help you understand how shut-off emotion manifests itself, let's look at its origin. If you are a victim, it was the *subconscious choice* you made in order to survive. Because the incestuous incident of abuse was so traumatic for you as a child or young person, it triggered a myriad of emotions. For the most part, these emotions are never openly expressed but pushed down and suppressed for years. This defense mechanism helped you deal with intense emotional pain, a pain so great that you learned to shut off the emotion associated with the incident. Whenever you began to feel it, you redirected your focus to something more pleasant. As years went by you learned through experience that this was an effective way to deal with unwanted emotion. I call it a survival technique because I learned from early childhood experiences how to survive my painful world. I learned that pain could be avoided by short-circuiting my emotions, and I learned not to deal with them. You must remember that for the victim this is not a conscious act, but through trial and error it becomes the best way to cope with life's circumstances.

Related to this shut-off of emotion is the victim who is very controlling. Most of these women appear strong and determined to control their environment. The controlling aspect of their personality has clearly evolved from their lack of control or powerlessness, in the abusive relationship. Many victims remember saying to themselves that they would never allow anyone to take advantage of them again. To understand how these two particular symptoms—shutting off emotions and the controlling personality—work together in the lives of victims, it is best to share experiences of real people.

Connie, a highly motivated woman in my first support group, decided it was time to get this "incest thing" taken care of. She was a dedicated Christian, well respected in her church. As the first few weeks went by, Connie was unable to get down to gut-level feelings. When she shared any details of her past, she presented them in an emotionless, matter-of-fact manner. The group encouraged her to allow her feelings to surface. Finally through some disturbing circumstances in her family, she got in touch with some emotion. As Connie met with her therapist and continued to receive support from the group, she learned how to get in touch with more of her feelings and even how to express them. She recognized that she had been denied the right to express any emotion as a child and she had carried this into her adult life.

Adele also was having difficulty feeling emotion about anything. She noticed this difficulty most in her inability to respond when someone told her, "I love you."

Adele said, "I can't even get the words out."

She struggled, too, with taking responsibility for everything. She tried to control her husband, her children, her environment and even her friends. She would make her wishes known and see to it that others conformed. Overall, she demonstrated strength and stoicism with limited compassion and sensitivity. Through the support group, Adele learned to trace the source of her behavior and to receive the encouragement she needed to change well-established patterns.

8. *Sexual problems in marriage.* As you see from the previous symptoms, one symptom seems to lead to another. I know of no victim who has not experienced some degree of sexual difficulties. It only makes sense that the wound inflicted in the past would show up again in this most intimate area. Many

husbands I counsel fail to see the connection at first. Often they respond by saying, "That was him back then and this is me now. Why is my wife still dwelling on the past?"

Dr. James Earnest, a clinical Christian psychologist with whom I worked, explains to the women in our groups that many sexual difficulties stem from flashbacks of the original incestuous incidents. He tells them it is much like the Vietnam veterans who experience what is known as Post-traumatic Stress Disorder. A similar situation may trigger what can be a devastating flashback. My own flashbacks demonstrated to me how dramatically and thoroughly the victim is affected. When in bed with my husband one evening I sensed his desire to be intimate. In the midst of lovemaking, I became rigid, frozen, unable to move. Because I had learned through therapy to process what was happening, I mentally investigated why I was reacting this way. Finally, after ruling out certain conditions in our environment, I hit on the cause of my intense reaction. It was my husband's after-shave. He was wearing the same fragrance my stepfather had worn for years. My subconscious had made the connection. When I've shared this example with victims, they invariably recall similar happenings.

As a victim you were attacked and violated in this area of intimacy and it is only logical that it bears some of the deepest scars. Sometimes victims are not aware of this problem. However, husbands report they sense a reservation or lack of interest by their wives. Jenny is a case in point. Prior to her coming to our group, Jenny and her husband had not been intimate in months. She shared with the other women, "I feel like an object, a non-person, every time he approaches me. I just can't fake it any longer." At one of our educational meetings conducted for husbands, we encouraged Jenny's husband to take time to just hug, caress, and hold his wife, nothing more. Like others before her, it was amazing how in a few months Jenny felt better about herself and about her husband. She was much freer to respond because she felt loved as a person and felt she had a choice in the intimate marital relationship.

The sexual problem in marriage is such a deep-rooted problem that it takes some time to work through. Some of the difficulty experienced by women in this area stems from guilt. As victims, children often feel some degree of physiological pleasure from the incestuous experience. Guilt over this causes them to shut off their pleasure mechanism and ultimately have difficulty experiencing enjoyment in their sexual relationship with their husbands. When I share this with victims they are relieved. They often feel they were the only ones who felt a physical response. I tell them that even at ten years of age, I felt my body respond physiologically. I, too, felt a great deal of guilt over this until I learned that God had made me a physiological being, equipped with natural, normal responses that would enable me to experience pleasure within the intimate relationship of marriage. Realizing that you are not responsible for these feelings and that their arousal was completely out of the context in which they were intended by God will help you place the responsibility where it belongs—with the aggressor. He activated those responses and it resulted in damage to you, the victim. As you share your experiences and your difficulties in this area, you can begin to break down the barriers that have isolated you from intimacy with your mate.

9. *Poor self-image/low self-esteem.* The foundational symptom suffered by all victims is their poor self-image. The two terms poor self-image and low self-esteem go hand in hand. When you work on one, the other improves.

Self-image is the view the victim holds of herself. From early years, she has internally viewed herself as bad or dirty, having little or no value. Unfortunately victims adopt a philosophy which says "bad things happen to bad people." Thus, when the incest occurs, the victim feels she deserved it, a conclusion not only due to the incest, but often due to the parenting she received and the overall family dynamics. Because she has a distorted view of her worth, the victim does not hold herself in very high regard, which in essence, is low self-esteem.

Do you focus on your failures rather than your success? Are you often skeptical and/or cynical and negative? Do you appear self-centered and introspective to others? Most incest victims do not feel good about themselves. Even those who appear confident and controlling may be victims of low self-esteem. Some have difficulty accepting criticism, and they become defensive. Others complacently accept whatever is dished out to them with an inability to stand up in their own behalf. They reject anything positive that is said about them. You might know someone like this. You might say to your friend Susan, "You got your hair cut—it sure looks nice that way."

Susan invariably replies, "Oh, I hate it. I should never have had it done." Or, "How can you say that? It looks awful today."

For years I constantly discredited positive feedback because I didn't feel good about myself. I had my own negative image. When people gave me positive strokes, their comments were incongruent with who I felt I was. I found ways to invalidate their feedback in order to keep my image intact. This, of course, was all on a subconscious level. I didn't recognize what I was doing.

Where does the victim's poor self-image come from? There is no doubt that the family plays a major role in the development of the child's self-image and self-esteem. In an incestuous family, there is always some type of dysfunction. Usually there is a breakdown between the husband and wife, which in turn is transmitted to the children. The parents are unable to love the child for who the child is, which results in the child's low self-esteem. It is obvious that any sexual contact between the victim and the aggressor further corroborates any negative feelings. When the victim is molested by a person outside the immediate family, the damage is just as devastating. I have worked with many women whose strong, supportive family built up their self-esteem as children. But after being victimized by someone outside the immediate family, their self-esteem suffered tremendously.

The self-image/self-esteem of an individual is at the foundation of who the person is. When that undergoes trauma or lack of proper development, it will show up in many areas. Picture the foundation of a home. If someone comes along and blows apart the foundation without the knowledge or consent of the builders, it will have a dramatic effect on the structure. Should the builders continue to build on such a foundation, the structure is destined to crumble. The incest victim's self-image is like that foundation, and when she tries to build her structure, her personality and character, on that faulty foundation, the signs of the damage eventually appear. She must go back to the foundation—the self-image—and restore it. Then she can go on to rebuilding the structure. Some of you are no doubt saying, "Not everyone who has a poor self-image is an incest victim." This, of course, is true. But I have yet to meet an incest victim who has not suffered from a poor self-image prior to obtaining counseling. In a later chapter we will discuss how this foundation can be rebuilt and what effect this will have on the victim and her relationship with others.

Additional Symptoms

I have covered what I regard as nine prominent symptoms. This is by no means an exhaustive list, for there are numerous physical, emotional, and spiritual symptoms which can be associated with victimization. Some of these include: migraine headaches, chronic inexplicable pain, and stomach ailments. Eating disorders such as anorexia (self-starvation), bulimia (binge eating and purging), compulsive eating, and obesity are symptomatic as well. Sleep disturbances such as insomnia, nightmares, and flashbacks are often reported by victims. Memory blocks or lapses in memory *may* be a sign of repression. Anxiety, panic attacks, and emotional outbursts may be experienced. A person who has experienced victimization may have difficulty trusting God and often feels undeserving of His love. A person who exhibits these and other symptoms should not make assumptions based on symptoms alone, but should seek qualified professional help to assist in the exploration of these presenting problems.

Teenage victims exhibit such things as promiscuity, running away from home, the choice of poor companions, drug and alcohol abuse, and an overall rebelliousness toward authority. A chaplain friend of mine, who surveyed female delinquents at a juvenile facility, found that as high as 90 percent had been molested as children. A Minneapolis survey of teenage prostitutes indicated 75 percent of them had been molested as children—leaving the perplexing question: "Why do victims become sexually promiscuous when they have been so traumatized by the molestation?"[6]

I have found that victims usually respond in one of three ways. First, they totally withdraw and have no desire to participate in any sexual relationship even within the context of marriage. Second, they respond by getting intimately involved with almost everyone they date prior to marriage, and often have affairs after marriage. Third, they respond erratically between the two. Often husbands report that one minute their wife will be extremely responsive and seductive and the next she will be cold, frigid and disinterested.

The key to understanding the promiscuous response lies in the tie the victim makes between love and sex. Many have paired the two. Thus, in order to feel loved, she engages in sex. For many victims the incestuous incident was the only time she felt loved. As I was growing up I was told that the only reason someone would be interested in me was for sexual reasons, leaving me with a distorted view of myself and my value as a person. It has been said that most prostitutes view themselves as objects and nonpersons. This, too, happens to the victim.

A second reason the victim may respond promiscuously is because of internal self-hatred. This is common in the teenage years. It is as if she is saying, "I'm damaged anyway, so I have no right to say no."

I have known several victims who, though promiscuous prior to marriage, become frigid and unresponsive after marriage. What happens? Prior to marriage the victim is trying desperately to feel loved. She jumps from one illicit relationship to another seeking that love which seems beyond her grasp. She is often involved with men who can only express tenderness and caring in a sexual setting, thus she finds herself in that setting much of the time. After the security of marriage, the ultimate question arises—will he still love me if I never have sex with him? The victim has incorrectly tied love and sex and, in order to reverse this tie, she thinks abstinence is the only solution. Of course, her husband has difficulty adjusting to her *uncommunicated* conclusion.

Personality traits such as being overly perfectionistic and/or rigid, a critical spirit, an inability to submit to authority and certain manipulative behaviors are all possible manifestations of an incestuous past. Unfortunately, a number of victims abuse their own children in some way, an astounding phenomenon. But again, the Scripture is clear that unless the sin is dealt with it can be carried from generation to generation. Victims do not want to abuse their children, but through the modeling they have received and the limited scope of their behavioral alternatives, they find themselves in the role of the aggressor.

Assessing Your Condition

In viewing these symptoms, don't jump to conclusions too rapidly. Should you see an overweight woman on the street corner who looks depressed, don't automatically assume she is an incest victim. It is the symptoms in combination that *may* be indicative of a traumatic past. Most of us have carried with us certain symptoms that have become part of who we are. Although I'd been mildly depressed for years, I'd never recognized it as a by-product of my past. I thought it was just the way I was. By addressing and working through my issues, I discovered joy and peace that I'd lived without for years.

Do you or does someone you know experience frequent periods of depression? Are you unreasonably angry with your husband and/or children? Do you feel intimidated or fearful around members of your family? Do you feel ashamed or intensely guilty when you have not met your expectations? Have you always had difficulty getting close to others or letting them get close to you? Do you find yourself being victimized repeatedly by others who impose their demands on you? Are you unable to cry or do you feel the need to control everything and everyone in your life? Do you enjoy your sexual relationship with your husband, or does the thought make you cringe at times? Can you accept a compliment graciously, or do you invalidate any positive strokes directed toward you?

If most of your answers are yes, I would challenge you to go back and read through the symptoms again. If you have no recollection of any sexual molestation in your childhood, yet you fit most of the symptoms, you may have repressed certain memories and you may need the help of a Christian professional to help you explore the symptom's roots. If you know you are a victim, realize that the symptoms you experience are shared by thousands of other women. You are not alone. Be honest with yourself. Be willing to face the problem by *examining yourself* as it says in 1 Corinthians 11:28. Just as with the destruction beneath the surface of the root-bound plant, your symptoms will not disappear on their own. You must be willing to dig up the past in order to experience health in the future. The Holy Spirit and the pages that follow will help you along the way. The process may be painful at times, but don't lose hope. The well-informed Gardener is urging you on. So am I.

PRACTICAL INSIGHTS

1. The Scripture says in 1 Corinthians 11:28: "Let a man examine himself." Below is a list of difficulties that you may be experiencing. Check any of the following that pertain to you:

    Headaches ☐   Low self-esteem ☐
    Guilt/shame ☐   Fear ☐
    Depression ☐   Sexual problems ☐
    Tiredness ☐   Loneliness ☐
    Memory blocks ☐   Nightmares ☐
    Isolation ☐   Anorexia ☐
    Panic attacks ☐   Bulimia ☐
    Anger ☐   Compulsiveness ☐
    Insomnia ☐   Lack of self-esteem ☐
    Anxiety ☐   Repeated victimization ☐
    Distance from God ☐

    Now that you have identified some of these difficulties, read Psalm 51:6. Over the next few months ask the Holy Spirit to begin revealing to you the truth about where these difficulties are rooted.

2. If you have checked seven or more of these items, it may be helpful for you to seek counseling from a Christian professional in your area.

3. Memorize John 8:32.

CHAPTER 3

Step II.

Recount the Incident

I can't do it," sobbed Mindy. "The words just won't come out. Are you sure this part is necessary?"

This is often the response I get from victims when we discuss the step of recounting. Although most victims can see incidents in their mind's eye, they often have difficulty verbalizing what they've experienced. You may ask, "Why *is* it necessary to verbalize trauma?" Have you ever been in an automobile collision? If you have, what is the first thing you do when you see a family member who wasn't present at the collision? You recount what happened. Why do you need to do that? It's because internal emotional energy is stored up inside of you and needs to be released. Talking about the incident doesn't change the event or its impact, but it does release some of the emotion surrounding your experience.

Most incest victims do not have the immediate opportunity to express their trauma to a supportive, nonjudgmental person. Instead, they hold the intense emotions surrounding the event inside and develop harmful defenses that allow them to cope with their internal pain. David Seamands writes that we have "the ability to block out of our minds things which we are not able to face. The saddest part of this is that though we may block out the pain quite unintentionally, we still suffer the consequences."[1]

Even when victims are afforded the opportunity to express

what has happened, guilt and self-incrimination make it difficult for them to verbalize their trauma. Mindy was a young woman in my support group whose life was laced with victimizations. We determined that incidents began with her father as early as when she was two or three. The sexual molestations were often accompanied by severe physical abuse and some deprivation. Mindy began pre-school at three years of age. She recalls, "I remember being taken into the principal's office one day. He often told me how pretty my hair was. The second or third time I was brought into his office, he began molesting me. These encounters lasted two or three years until we moved away. The principal made me do all sorts of things to him as well. I felt that I had no one to turn to." Later in Mindy's life she was molested by her older brother, her cousin and an uncle.

It wasn't until Mindy was married and had children that God showed her that she needed to work through the issues of her past. Because of the extent of victimization and the early age at which it began, Mindy's healing process will be a lengthy one. However, she has made considerable progress even in a six-month period. In a case such as Mindy's, I'm often asked if it is necessary for the victim to recount every single incident. I believe it is important for her to verbalize the emotions and feelings associated with every incident that comes to mind. She may find later, that additional incidents will surface; these will need to be dealt with then.

What Does Recounting Accomplish?

Even after I had completed therapy and was leading support groups, I realized the importance of this step of recounting. I had one memory that I never verbalized because it seemed insignificant in light of my other recollections. One evening while being intimate with my husband, I was unable to respond to him. I realized that my husband was touching me in the same way my stepdad had. I instantly flashed back for a moment to when I was fourteen. A few nights later, with my head nestled in my husband's arms, for the first time I recounted what I had experienced at fourteen. I began to sob and immediately felt the release of the internal pressure and false guilt that I had been carrying for fifteen years. Each time I shared this experience with women in our support groups, I felt a little less bound by the memory until I could recount the event without the shame that I had sentenced myself to for all those years.

I realized then that Satan capitalizes on the emotional hurts in our lives and keeps us in a state of condemnation when, instead, we could be walking in liberation due to Christ's complete work on the cross.

Stormie Omartian, a victim of severe child abuse, once said at a seminar, "Satan sets out to conceal, but God is a revealer of truth."

Recounting the incident allows the victim to begin to release some of the emotions around her experience and brings to light that which has been hidden so long.

Is There Scriptural Basis?

Recounting the incident is often a controversial issue in Christian circles. Often people quote such verses as 2 Corinthians 5:17: "Old things have passed away; behold, all things have become new;" or Philippians 3:13: "But one thing I do, forgetting those things which are behind and reaching forward to those things which are ahead. . . ." If we look at the preceding verses in chapter 3 of Philippians, we find Paul recounting some of his past. Paul never forgot where he came from, including how he was actively involved in persecuting the church. The emphasis of Paul's instruction is not to dwell on the past in such a way that we are ineffective in the present. For the victim, it is extremely important that she look in depth at her experience because she has spent a lifetime avoiding the pain.

When I began asking the Lord to show me Scripture that demonstrated this principle, the Lord led me to study the book of Nehemiah. Nehemiah had a burden to rebuild the wall in Jerusalem. He obtained permission from the king to go to Jerusalem. In Nehemiah 2:11-18 we read that he rose up in the night and began an expedition to survey the wall. He went from gate to gate viewing that which had been broken down and destroyed. After doing that, he gathered the men together and shared his vision and plan for rebuilding.

Victims need to follow Nehemiah's example. They must survey the losses and damage in their lives before they can intelligently set about to rebuild. This process may be a lengthy one because the damage has been extensive. As a counselor, I walk victims through their surveying stage, assist them with their rebuilding blueprint, and help them begin to implement their plan for recovery.

Many times Christians prematurely instruct those who have experienced a tremendous loss to "move on." We decide for victims that they have spent enough time dwelling on the past, but we can do damage by our chastisement. A willingness to let them move ahead more slowly would be much more helpful. There is an appropriate time to encourage a person who is wallowing in self-pity to look ahead and move on with life, but there is a difference between surveying a loss that has deeply affected your entire being and dwelling on the past in a negative, self-destructive way.

By recounting the incidents and building on a Scriptural foundation, the victim can receive feedback that is valuable to her recovery. However, I stress that, if the victim has kept her experience secret since she was a child, she be careful to share this information with the right person. To choose someone who is not supportive or empathetic can cause further damage. I recommend that women share with someone they *know* will respond with a deep understanding and acceptance—one who will not blame, condemn, judge, or gloss over what has happened. Unfortunately, many women cannot go to their husbands or pastors because these men will not provide the support needed. Too often well-meaning Christians, even pastors, tell victims they need to move on, quit dwelling on the past, and simply be obedient to the Word. It is just not that simple!

How to Recount

Now that we have laid the groundwork for recounting the incidents, let's discuss how this is done. It is often necessary for a victim to discuss some family history or family dynamics in order for the victimization to be seen in context. The incest was not an isolated event that sprang up from a normal, healthy home environment. Instead, it was a product of a dysfunctional, unhealthy home or set of interpersonal relationships. It will probably help at this point to share my own story.

I felt a great deal of isolation as a child and a deep sense of rejection. Love was not demonstrated in our home through hugs or open affection. I was the youngest of three girls. Saundra was seven years my senior and Kathy was four years older. Our mother married at fifteen to our natural father who was ten years her senior. In my early years we had a live-in housekeeper because my mother worked. Then, as you know, when I was five my parents divorced.

After the divorce, the isolation increased. I longed for acceptance and approval in school, yet I was keenly aware of rejection and wished to avoid it at almost any cost. My mother, the family's sole supporter, left us on our own a great deal. When I was seven, my oldest sister got married and left the home. During that time, my mother was dating George, the man who would later become my stepfather. I can recall two specific incidents that were demonstrations of the dysfunctional aspects of our home. The first was a day when my mom allowed George to take pictures of all of us lying nude on her bed. Even though I was only seven, I felt embarrassed about being undressed in front of a man I didn't know very well. I also vividly remember my mother asking us girls to choose between George and another man she was dating. We chose George and they were married when I was eight.

George was sharply different from my natural father. George was a strict disciplinarian, rigid in authority—and our submission was an absolute must. Though he was a Christian and the church we began attending was a fundamental, Bible-believing church, he was intolerant and inflexible. During the first year or two of their marriage, George volunteered to give us showers. My mother encouraged this activity and this was the beginning of some subtle sexual overtures. My stepfather and mother also began putting pressure on us to discontinue seeing our natural father. They would degrade him and emotionally punish us whenever we expressed a desire to see him. Due to that pressure, we chose not to see him anymore. This illustrates the isolation that is so common in incestuous homes. The family becomes insulated, a closed system that has little interaction with the outside environment. Loyalty to the immediate family becomes the motto and goal, and must be sustained at all costs. Researchers are finding this closed system concept substantiated in many studies of incestuous homes.

While attending our church, I began to feel loved and accepted for the first time in my life. I heard about Jesus who loved me so much that He died for me. During one evening service I went forward and asked Christ to come into my life. That was life-changing for me. Three weeks later, my mother and sister attended a mother-daughter tea at church leaving my baby brother and me at home with George. I had gone to bed when my stepfather called me out into the living room and told me I could sit on the couch and watch TV with him. As we were watching TV, he unzipped his clothing and told me to lie between his legs and rub him. It seemed to last an eternity. He then made me lie on top of him and he went through the motions of intercourse, but because my underpants were on, penetration was not achieved. I felt numb as he sent me off to bed that night cautioning me not to tell my mother because she would be very angry with me.

Alone in my cold, dark bedroom I felt fearful, confused and guilty. I experienced vaginal contractions and it frightened me. I immediately felt guilty, assuming that, since my body had responded, I must have been responsible for what had occurred. It was not until years later that I realized God had made me a normal, complete physiological being, and He had made me in such a way that I would respond, but His design for that response was only within the bond of marriage. My stepfather had activated my God-given response system, but outside of God's order and timing. The guilt I felt when it happened was a false guilt, but it still caused many difficulties later in my life and marriage.

About a month after the molestation, my mother came to me and asked if George had ever touched me. I said yes and described what had taken place. She didn't ask me anything else and I never heard another word about it. I did not realize it at the time, but George was continually molesting my older sister, Kathy. Kathy went to my mother, but was not believed. Yet this is what had prompted my mother to question me.

Over the next eleven years, there were several times when he touched and kissed me inappropriately. He and my mother had me watch them have intercourse as part of my sex education, and they never allowed me any privacy. While these things were upsetting to me, the incident at ten seemed, at the time, to have the most devastating effect. Many times women will diminish their experiences by saying, "Oh, it wasn't that bad." I have found, however, through personal experience and in working with hundreds of victims, that even the most minor of incidents can carry with it a profound, life-changing effect. Of course, the duration and extensiveness of the abuse, coupled with the degree of closeness of the offender to the victim, will affect the extent of devastation.

I went through some difficult periods during that time as my mother suffered an injury that caused her to be hospitalized for a lengthy period. One of my most fearful memories had to do with the year my mother was in and out of the hospital. One Friday evening my stepfather took my sister and me to a drive-in movie entitled, "How to Murder Your Wife," starring Jack Lemmon. If you saw that movie, you know it is a spoof intended to be extremely funny. But I sat in that car petrified, convinced that George went only to see how he could murder my mother. I fell asleep that night fearing that I would have to live with my stepfather the rest of my life.

To many, this fear may seem unrealistic, but for a child of ten, it was very real. We often do a disservice to victims by discounting or intellectualizing their experiences, forgetting that little children's fears, confusions and doubts are very real. Children do not have all the sophisticated defense mechanisms we adults create. Children's emotions are essentially "in the raw." As we will see in the following chapter, it is important for the victim to tap into her childlike feelings enroute to a healthy resolution.

During my later elementary and junior-high-school years, I went through some dramatic personality changes. I went from being an outgoing leader to a withdrawn, self-conscious young girl. At that time I did not attribute any of those changes to my experience. In fact, I suppressed the molestation for seventeen years. That is not to say that it did not affect my daily life. It did! I was just not aware of the impact it was having.

In high school I was involved in many activities and was a high achiever. I realize now that my busyness kept me from feeling too much pain, and my achievements became the sole source of my self-esteem. God was certainly gracious to me during that time, as I was fortunate enough to never have experimented with drugs or alcohol. I did, however, begin a destructive cycle in my relationships.

During my late adolescence I became involved in a series of emotionally abusive relationships and was rebellious toward my parents. As I look back now, though, I am able to see how much of my behavior stemmed from my experiences as a child, even with regard to my chosen profession. I always had a desire to work with troubled young people.

After graduation from college with a B.A. in psychology, I began working for the Probation Department as a counselor at a juvenile hall. I spent two years working with abused, neglected and delinquent children and young people, ranging in age from birth to eighteen years. I spent the next five years as a Probation Officer working with both juvenile and adult offenders. I wish I had known then what I know now! Some research indicates that as high as nine out of ten girls in juvenile facilities have been molested as children. It was during this juvenile hall experience, at the age of twenty-one, that I realized for the first time that what my stepfather had done to me was a criminal act.

In my early twenties I recommitted my life to Christ and asked the Lord to help me forgive my stepfather for what he had done. I thought at that point I had resolved it, but it wasn't until after I was married that the Lord revealed to me that these hurts had never been resolved. I struggled with many issues, including why it was necessary for me to bring up all the pain of my past. I searched the Scripture for answers.

I was reminded of Jesus' encounter with the Samaritan woman at the well in John 4. In verse 16 Jesus focuses on a present-day issue in the life of this woman. He says to her, "Go, call your husband and come here." Her immediate response is, "I have no husband." Jesus replies, "You have well said, 'I have no husband,' for you have had five husbands, and the one whom you now have is not your husband; in that you spoke truly" (4:17). Later in verses 28 and 29 we read that the woman left her waterpot, went into the city and told the people to "Come, see a Man who told me all things that I ever did."

Jesus used *recounting* as a means of addressing past and present issues in this needy woman's life. Perhaps this conversation was more lengthy than what is recorded in Scripture. It is my supposition that Jesus spent a great deal of time with the woman recounting past events that no doubt contributed to where she was that day. There is no way that we can know how long they talked, but we do know that the woman was so struck with all that Jesus said that, through her experience, she and many others came to know him as Messiah.

Recounting the incident is not a magical cure. It is a vital step in the process, which allows the victim to gain momentum and gives substance to previously confusing unexplored emotions. Recounting not only helps the victim to gain perspective of her past, but it also enables her to address present issues.

As we have seen, recounting the experience is valuable for the victim—it has a scriptural basis and is the impetus for future change. It is often a painful step because it unlocks deep, intense emotions that imprison the victim in her adult life. It is because of this imprisonment that the feelings must be brought to the surface, experienced, and ultimately released. We will examine this step thoroughly in the following chapter.

PRACTICAL INSIGHTS

1. Write in detail at least one incident involving some deep hurt you experienced in your childhood. Which of the following ways did you respond to that hurt?

Acted like I was not hurt	☐	Withdrew	☐
Cried	☐	Told someone	☐
Felt rejected/embarrassed	☐	Felt responsible	☐
Got angry Other	☐	Other	☐

    As you reflect on yourself today, what similarities do you find between how you handled hurt in the past and how you handle it now?

2. Read Nehemiah 2:11-18. As you begin to survey the losses in your life, as Nehemiah did, you will be better equipped to rebuild your life intelligently.

3. Memorize Isaiah 41:10.

CHAPTER 4

Step III.

Experience the Feelings

C oleen came to our support group after hearing me speak at a church brunch. Previously we had several phone conversations about the goals and benefits of such a group for victims. During those conversations she had commented, "I have worked through most everything that you have talked about, but I would still like to be a part of your upcoming group." Because I did not sense in her the level of resolution that she purported to have, I encouraged her to join us.

As Coleen and the other five women all made self-introductions, I noted Coleen's rambling speech. She was by no means incoherent, but she was redundant and she seemed to have a need to talk incessantly. It was apparent that she had worked through some issues with regard to being victimized, but I felt she subconsciously was trying to cover up a hidden reservoir of emotions. After four or five weeks in the group, Coleen announced that she was ready to confront her parents. We explored her reasons for doing this and each group member gave feedback about her plan. I sensed that she was just not ready for this confrontation and in a gentle way expressed this to her. I told her I didn't believe she had ever really *experienced* the deep emotion she had felt as a child and that this step was essential in the recovery process. I suggested that she

45

wait at least one week and that we both pray about her decision.

When I walked into the group the following Tuesday, Coleen was slumped over in a chair with her face buried in her hands, sobbing uncontrollably. "What's wrong?" I asked as I wrapped my arms around her.

"I've been crying for five days straight. I can't believe the beautician did this to me. She betrayed me and I'm so angry!" Between sobs Coleen related to the group how she'd gone to a particular beauty salon at the recommendation of a friend. She took a picture of the haircut style she wanted and showed it to the beautician. Coleen said, "I was horrified when I looked at what she'd done. She totally disregarded my request and cut off way too much. I went home in tears and as I stroked the back of my hair, I became more infuriated. I couldn't stop crying and my husband had trouble understanding why this was such a big deal. As I looked in the mirror at home, it hit me. My hair looked exactly like it did when I was thirteen, the year my dad molested me. The sense of betrayal I felt toward the beautician reminded me of the feelings I had toward my dad. It's been almost a week since I got my hair cut and I can't stop crying. I can't believe this is happening to me — I've never been so out of control with my emotions. What can I do to make myself stop?"

"Coleen," I responded tenderly, "you are grieving over a loss, a loss that your inner child was never allowed to grieve over. You have carried these deep emotions all these years and God is using this present experience to allow you to get in touch with your pain. Don't shut it off. Allow yourself to release these feelings. I'm not sure how long it will take, but I promise you, it won't last forever."

Coleen went away that night, hopeful even in the midst of her pain. She cried for another week, but later reported that the experience was the turning point in her recovery. She has since confronted her parents and restoration is taking place in her family.

Experiencing feelings is important for anyone who has suffered an emotional hurt. Unfortunately the Christian community often advises us to ignore, gloss over, or put aside our feelings. This can be unwise as our feelings have a way of creeping out anyway, and in ways that can be destructive.

A friend I'll call Denise found this to be true in her situation. She'd been married three years when she learned her husband was having an affair. Several well-meaning Christian friends told her that the "godly" thing to do was to forgive her husband and go on as if this had never happened. Denise genuinely tried to do this but she soon found that she was suspicious if her husband came home late from the office. Often she'd search his pockets under the guise of preparing them for laundering. She would watch him with a critical eye around other women. After Denise came to me, I encouraged her to identify and experience the original feelings of betrayal and anger she'd felt over her husband's unfaithfulness, and even to share those feelings with him. It was not a one-time event but something they worked on for months. Denise is convinced now, five years later, that this was a vital step in the healing of her marriage. She says, "Had I not faced and worked through those intense feelings, I know we would not be together today. Because I worked through those emotions, they no longer creep out in suspiciousness and distrust, and the love for my husband has been restored."

Are Feelings Important?

Some of you may be asking, "How do I begin to experience my feelings?" As stated in the previous chapter, the first step is finding an appropriate person with whom to share your feelings. Often victims think that if they begin to get in touch with these deep emotions, they will end up going off the deep end. This is rarely the case, but it is beneficial to have the expertise of a specialized therapist when dealing with these intense emotions. I recommend that victims obtain several Christian counseling referrals from a reputable church in their area. I then suggest they contact several therapists and specifically ask them about their expertise in the area of victimization. It is usually safe to say that those who lead therapy groups for victims are specialists. I encourage the victim then to go to the counselor she feels most comfortable with over the phone.

After a victim has found a knowledgeable therapist, she needs to relive at least one incident in the past and try to express the feelings she felt as a child. This may take a period of time. If you, as a victim, are having difficulty feeling any emotions, it might be helpful to dig out old pictures and draw floor plans of the home in which you lived at the time of the molestation. Take these into the therapeutic setting as a catalyst to trigger some of those lost feelings.

I caution you not to do this on your own. These are therapeutic techniques that are best implemented under the supervision and direction of a professional. If verbalization of these feelings is particularly difficult, a preliminary step of journalizing may be helpful. While in counseling, I found that writing at home was very therapeutic for me and I sometimes read aloud what I had written. It is often difficult for victims to express feelings they have never labeled. Writing about your experiences and feelings of the present helps you define and label feelings from the past. This technique is helpful for anyone who has experienced an emotional wound. Being able to express and deal with our feelings can set us free from the binding-up that often occurs when we hold things inside.

In his book, *Understanding Your Past — the Key to Your Future*, Dr. Cecil Osborne writes, "Feelings do not age. Feelings about past events are in us now.... Time does not diminish childhood hurts. ... They do not erode or disappear."[1] I have seen this confirmed over and over in the lives of women who were not given the opportunity to release justified emotion at the time they experienced a trauma.

Our Child Within

The concept of the child within us may need some explanation at this point. All of us have within ourselves a childlike part. When we reach adulthood, we do not automatically disengage from all events, feelings, and experiences that were uniquely part of our childhood. If we, as children, experienced events that in some way damaged our emotions, and those issues and feelings were not resolved, we carry them into adulthood. In his book, *Your Inner Child of the Past*, W. H. Missildine states, "You must learn to recognize these feelings and childhood longings as important, deserving of respect and separate from your adult feelings."[2] When we continue to carry these feelings around with us as adults, we will often experience frustration, anxiety and hopelessness. I have used the example of a reservoir. When we carry that reservoir of emotion, it eventually fills and spills over, often in an uncontrollable fashion. We can deliberately begin to open a floodgate of feelings, releasing some of the emotion and reducing the danger of uncontrolled spillage.

As I share the concept of the child within each of us with men and women, it often becomes apparent that the child's needs of healthy love and affection were not met. This, of course, occurs in other than incestuous homes. Unfortunately, it is a widespread phenomenon. Many children grow up to be needy adults in search of a love they never knew as children. This is tragic, as it seems to be passed from generation to generation. It is no wonder we face an epidemic of teen suicide in this country. Children need a healthy sense of love! I was moved to tears when I heard a song written by Steve and Annie Chapman. The lyrics seem so appropriate to those of us who were denied a healthy love:

> *Daddy, you're the man in your little girl's dreams,*
> *you are the one she longs to please.*
> *And there's a place in her heart*
> *that can only be filled*
> *with her daddy's love.*
> *But if you don't give her the love she desires,*
> *she'll try someone else,*
> *but they won't satisfy'er.*
> *And if your little girl grows up without Daddy's love,*
> *she may feel empty and it's only because*
> *it's her daddy's love that she's looking for,*
> *don't send her away to another man's door.*
> *Nobody else can do what you do,*
> *she just needs her daddy's love.*
> *And someday if you hear her purity's gone,*
> *she may have lost it tryin' to find*
> *what was missing at home.*
> *Just let the heavenly Father*
> *heal where you fail,*
> *He can forgive you and help you to give her*
> *the daddy's love that she's looking for,*
> *don't send her away to another man's door.*
> *Nobody else can do what you do,*
> *she just needs her daddy's love.*
> *You know it's true,*
> *she just needs her daddy's love.*[3]

If only dads everywhere would realize the need in their little girl's heart for that *healthy* love. It is important to note that our child within us need not hurt forever. We can learn how to nurture the child within ourselves through God's healing love. I will discuss this concept further in a later chapter.

I discovered the importance of releasing the emotions of the child within me during my therapy. Although my therapist and I had not discussed this concept, I remember I had a significant breakthrough in the midst of my therapy process. I went to bed one evening with much on my mind — dealing with a lot of emotion, trying to filter through my thoughts and feelings, and praying, asking the Lord how I would ever be able to get over the pain I was feeling. As I lay in bed that night, I began sobbing uncontrollably. In a barely audible, childlike voice I cried out, "Leave me alone; I'm only ten years old. Please . . . I don't understand." I repeated this several times and felt a flood of emotion being released. It seemed like I cried for hours. I didn't realize how significant this was until I went back to therapy the following week and gained new insight into the pain I had felt as a child. That release of emotion seemed to unlock areas that had been bound up. I had always had trouble expressing love and receiving it from my husband. I noticed that after this experience I was able to be more aware of my own feelings and had a better ability to express them to Don.

This area of experiencing the feelings is very important in the healing process. It includes experiencing feelings both past and present and is vitally significant for the victim who has shut off her emotion. She has learned to do this as a means to survive. The shut-off primarily occurs as a result of dealing with intense pain. The child adopts this technique as a way to cope emotionally. Unfortunately, this pattern is often carried into adulthood and can severely affect a woman's relationships. These women are often in denial. Many times it is necessary to teach them how to identify their emotions in the present before they can connect with their feelings of the past and with their child within.

Luci was a perfect example. She would describe in detail how someone in her church had mistreated her and as she spoke I observed "fire" in her eyes. I commented that it sounded like she was really mad at what this person had done. She quickly corrected me and said, "Oh, no, Jan, it doesn't bother me at all." Luci had to begin recognizing her coping mechanism of denial and learn to allow herself to express emotion in the present before she could deal with past issues.

Another woman, Bonnie, exemplified this shut-off in a different way. She was an angry woman who often screamed and swore about both present-day events and the past abuse she had suffered as a child at the hands of her father. One evening our support group discussed the need of tapping into the anger, confusion and fear felt in childhood in order to release it. Bonnie piped up and said, "I have no trouble with that! In fact, I am tired of being angry. I have been angry as long as I can remember and it's interfering with my life."

I looked at Bonnie and said, "Bonnie, there's another whole side to your child within which you've never known. It's the vulnerable, fearful child who is in need of love and nurturing. I sense for you that your intense anger is a cover-up to avoid that vulnerable deep fear that you felt so long ago." Bonnie started to cry, then asked, "Isn't there any other way? I don't want to go back through that fear and pain. I'll do anything to avoid that."

Truth Sets Us Free

To those of you who are asking that very same question, the answer is no, at least on a human level there is no other way. I do not ever wish to limit God and His power to help us, but I have found that, outside of His intervention, avoiding those feelings only intensifies their impact and bondage. Jesus said in John 8:32, "You shall know the truth, and the truth shall make you free." The truth is often painful, but it is in finding, facing and feeling that truth that we can begin to rebuild our lives. Jesus said in John 16:33, "In the world you will have tribulation; but be of good cheer, I have overcome the world."

As we discussed in the previous chapter, Nehemiah grieved over the loss at Jerusalem. His grief became a prerequisite and the motivating force behind his determination to rebuild the wall. Going from gate to gate, processing his grief, he carefully surveyed the destruction and examined the extent of the damage. As victims, we must feel the feelings and scrutinize the loss resulting from the injury. But our focus must not remain there. We are to assess the damage in order to plan wisely for the future restoration. We must look carefully at the losses and feelings we experienced in childhood traumas in order to gather the material needed to begin a rebuilding program.

One of my favorite Scripture verses, which I often pray for myself and encourage other victims to pray, is Psalm 51:6: "Behold, You desire truth in the inward parts,/ And in the hidden part You will make me to know wisdom." God knows our inward parts and He desires that we deal with what is true. It is not healthy for us to pretend these events did not happen or to deny the devastation that has resulted. I am encouraged when women begin to deal with the hurts of their past. In Psalm 44:21 we read: "Would not God search this out?/ For He knows the secrets of the heart." Are you struggling with some of these secret feelings? Are you doubting whether or not to explore them further? Or are you feeling guilty over your inability to resolve this on your own? Then read on! The next step of establishing responsibility will begin to open your "door of hope"!

PRACTICAL INSIGHTS

1. Refer to the incident you described in detail at the end of the previous chapter. As you reflect on your *feelings* at the time of that incident, which ones do you remember experiencing? (People often have more than one feeling at a time and sometimes these feelings seem like opposites, i.e., love/hate.)

Embarrassment ☐	Confusion ☐	Frustration ☐
Shame ☐	Sadness ☐	Shyness ☐
Anger ☐	Hate ☐	Approval ☐
Resentment ☐	Happiness ☐	Guilt ☐
Rejection ☐	Warmth ☐	
Love ☐	Fear ☐	

2. Read Isaiah 53:2-5. Jesus was acquainted with grief and sorrow. He understands the depths of your emotion and He accepts you fully.

3. Memorize Hebrews 4:15.

CHAPTER 5

Step IV:

Establish Responsibility

In his book, *Love Must Be Tough*, Dr. James Dobson writes, "If there is anything that an adulterer does not need, it is a guilt-ridden mate who understands his indiscretion and assumes the blame for it. Such a person needs to be called to accountability, not excused by rationalization."[1] Let me change two words in that short quote: "If there is anything that an *aggressor* does not need, it is a guilt-ridden *victim* who understands his indiscretion and assumes the blame for it. Such a person needs to be called to accountability, not excused by rationalization." Recognizing the need for this accountability, or establishing responsibility, is a crucial step in overcoming the symptoms associated with victimization.

One of the main difficulties a victim has in calling the aggressor to accountability is her own self-judgment at being a co-participant in the incestuous act. As we discussed in chapter 1, the victim tends to assume some of the responsibility herself for her victimization.

Paula's Story

I will never forget Paula, a young woman in my support group. Paula's natural father died of cancer when she was nine years old. Paula described the great loss she felt. "We were so close and always did a lot of fun things together. My mother and I were never close like my dad and me. When he died I felt like I'd lost my best friend. I remember crying for months on end."

Because of the financial pressures, her mother sent Paula to live with an uncle and aunt after her father died. Her uncle started taking her places and trying to fill the vacancy her father had left. She remembered climbing up into her uncle's lap before bedtime each evening. "Then," she said, "something changed. One evening my uncle asked me to come and sit in his lap like always. As I sat there I felt his hand begin to creep into my pajama bottoms. I was so frightened, but he assured me that I was his special girl and that he just wanted to show me how much he loved me. He told me my aunt would not understand and would send me away if I ever told her. I never did. Now I am so ashamed. If I hadn't needed so much affection as a child, I wouldn't have climbed into his lap, and it never would have happened."

Paula had made some faulty assumptions. First, she assumed that her need for affection had prompted her uncle's actions. Second, she assumed that the incident would have been avoided if she hadn't climbed into her uncle's lap. Both assumptions presume that Paula is responsible for her uncle's actions.

The truth is: a child victim is 100 percent free of any responsibility. *The aggressor is always fully responsible.* We have been duped often by society into thinking that the "seductive child" is merely getting what she asks for. This is false. I do not believe there is any such child walking around, but even if there were, the adult still holds complete responsibility for his behavior. My experience has taught me that a child who is behaving in a sexually precocious manner usually has been molested already. A victim of child molestation suffers from having her sexual arousal system activated prematurely. This causes confusion, misunderstanding, and a sexual identity imbalance in the child. She is forced to deal with emotions and physiological responses that God did not intend for her to experience until the pubertal years. It is no wonder victims suffer difficulty in later years.

For Paula, it was necessary to go back in time and look at the child within her. She had never come to grips with the enormous loss she suffered at the death of her father, and she never had an opportunity to express her angry feelings of being deserted and betrayed when he died. Then her uncle committed the ultimate betrayal. He capitalized on the trusting relationship he had created, and robbed Paula of her dignity, her self-respect, and her right to be loved appropriately. In light of these traumatic events, her nine-year-old personality told her there must be something terribly bad about her for these two significant men in her life to betray her.

We counseled with Paula a great deal, allowing her to work through her emotions. Finally she came to the point where she could release herself of responsibility and bring her uncle to accountability. It was important to help Paula see that there was nothing she could have done to prevent the aggressor's actions.

Many victims attempt to find every loophole in order to absolve their aggressor from responsibility. There is a point at which compassion and understanding become a part of the total resolution for the victim, but, in these early stages, the victim must not rationalize away the accountability of the offender.

Fear of Loss

The next reason a victim has difficulty establishing responsibility is her fear of losing valued relationships. Some victims have no desire to have a relationship with the one who has offended them. Others, however, feel pressured to maintain a relationship due to loyalty issues within the family. This often prevents the victim from establishing proper accountability.

This predicament was illustrated in the life of a young woman named Ruthie. Ruthie had been molested from the time she was five until she was twelve by her older brother Peter. She had suffered physical abuse perpetrated by him as well. Her father was an alcoholic and her mother worked two jobs to support the family. Her mother would come and praise Peter for "being so responsible" by taking care of his little sister. Her mother would then turn to Ruthie and say, "Your brother is such a good boy. Now Ruthie, you make sure you mind your brother today like a good girl." Ruthie felt powerless. As the years went by, her mother never looked into the pain that was evident in Ruthie's eyes. She just kept right on patting Peter on the back and as Ruthie once told me, "I could never tell my mother what he did. She would never believe me, and even if she did, it would tear our family apart. I know my mother couldn't handle it."

Unfortunately victims are in a double bind. They feel guilty for not telling parents, teachers, or someone in authority; yet they cannot tell because it could disrupt the family unit and they would feel guilty about that. Often these feelings are carried over into adult life and play a significant role in the recovery process.

Co-contributors

It is important at this point to discuss other responsible parties. I am referring to anyone (besides the aggressor) who may not be a direct participant but who has knowledge of the molestation, or sees signs of such. That person is a co-contributor.

It is difficult to establish the responsibility of other members without knowing each individual case. I do not wish to pronounce judgment on anyone who may be struggling with these things. However, it is important to consider prayerfully the accountability issue, not for the purpose of blaming, but to correctly establish responsibility.

In most cases of father-daughter incest, which also would include a stepfather or any male assuming the paternal role in the household, the mother holds a *measure* of responsibility and is therefore a co-contributor. *The measure or amount is variable depending upon the specifics of each individual case.* In my own experience, my mother held a significant measure of responsibility. She allowed my stepdad to take pictures of us nude as children, even before they were married. After their marriage, she encouraged me to take showers with George because, according to her, "He always does such a good job of shampooing your hair." She modeled a helplessness that made me, as a child, realize that if she was helpless, I most certainly was helpless. She often mediated between my stepdad and us which contributed to the isolation between family members, so typical in incestuous homes.

Until I started therapy, I was totally unaware of the anger I felt toward my mother. Out of my fear of losing the only valuable parental relationship I thought I had, I remained in denial over my mother's role for years. I saw my mother as victimized by my stepfather's emotional abuse. It was impossible to establish her accountability—until I realized she had made choices, a painful revelation for me. One day during a therapy session I blurted out, "I guess what hurts the most is that she made a choice for him over me and she continued to make that choice over and over again."

Once I was able to look at my mother's responsibility, I no longer felt that pressure to hold the family together. It freed me from that and allowed me to look at my relationship with my mother realistically. Even as an adult, I set expectations for my mother that were unrealistic. Not that they were beyond her ability to achieve, but they were incongruent with her past behavior. Let me illustrate.

Prior to my first daughter's birth I asked my mother to come and stay with us a few days when we came home from the hospital. All my girl friends' mothers had jumped excitedly at the opportunity to come into their homes for a week and take over the meals and housecleaning and to try out their new roles as grandmas. When I asked my mother, she hesitated. "Well, I don't know," she said. "You know your dad and brother need me here to take care of things." I was crushed and she knew it. A few days later she called and said, "Your dad is mad about it, but I just told him I was going to come down when the baby arrives." Heather was born on a Saturday and we went home on Monday afternoon. My mother arrived early Tuesday morning and stayed until Thursday. All along I had expected her to spend four or five days with us. I was so hurt when she left after two days that it triggered the same feelings I had as a child—that my stepdad's needs and desires came before mine.

In therapy I saw how I continually set myself up for rejection from my mother. I began to analyze my relationship with her and I realized it lacked a very vital component: openness. Our relationship remained intact largely due to my efforts and my ability to stay within the parameters my mother had defined. For us there were two criteria for maintaining a harmonious relationship. First, I could not discuss the molestation or any injustices I had felt as a child. Second, I was not to mention my natural father. As long as I kept within those limits, our relationship went along fairly smoothly. Mother often confided in me regarding my stepdad's unjust behavior toward her and toward my brother. But I was never to draw comparisons about his treatment of me or suggest she take some action. I was merely to listen and feel sympathetic for her position.

Family Denial

The realization that she had made choices in the past and was continuing to make choices helped me understand that, as an adult, I, too, had the right to make decisions on my own behalf. I decided to deal openly with my mother regardless of the consequences. My first step toward openness was to share with my mother regarding the emotional difficulties I was having due to the incest. This prompted me to have no contact with my stepdad for about a year.

This sharing caused a strain in my relationship with my mother, but I was no longer in denial. I was unwilling to pretend, even with her, that the molestation never happened. It might help to illustrate it this way:

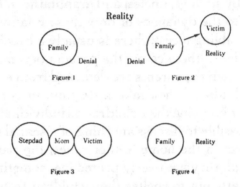

In many incestuous families it is very common for all members to remain in a denial sphere, as shown in Figure 1. Each party knows what occurred, but continues to act as if it never happened. If a victim begins to face what has happened she may remove herself to the reality sphere, as in Figure 2. All other members, however, may choose to continue in their denial. In my case, I had crossed over to the reality sphere. My father remained in denial and my mother attempted to be a mediating bridge between the two worlds. Whenever she was with me, she was forced to touch reality, but at home with my stepdad, she remained in touch with denial, as seen in Figure 3. Ultimately, for any type of restoration for the entire family to occur all parties must be willing to work with the reality sphere, as illustrated in Figure 4. The step from denial to reality is achieved through confrontation. This is discussed at length in Chapter Nine. But remember, the victim can experience restoration even if all other family members are unwilling to face reality.

Other Co-contributors

We have primarily focused on the role of the mother as co-contributor. Who else might be considered a co-contributor? I have had numerous women come to me who have been victimized by siblings, uncles, and grandfathers. Many factors contribute to the dynamics of how these relationships begin. In cases of sibling incest, there is usually a breakdown in the parental role. In these cases, the parents become the co-contributors. Often the parents are detached from each other and from the children. They take little time in communicating, observing or knowing their children as individuals. They often find it impossible to discuss anything of a sexual nature; it is a taboo subject in the home. Other times, the parents are extremely rigid; they are overly protective, sometimes religious types who attempt to shelter their children from the evils of everything from commercials to ice cream. I am not inferring that we do not need to protect our children. However, in the families that take this to extreme, it creates an isolationism of the family, which tends to foster the incestuous atmosphere.

Kantor and Lehr (1975), family researchers, describe these family types as being the "closed systems" we mentioned earlier.[2] They are not open to involvement with the outside world. Arlene came from this type of family. Her parents were rigid, legalistic church people. She had four brothers and two sisters. She was the middle girl. Her parents were upstanding people who made certain their children avoided the contamination of the school system by keeping them home, forbade them to watch TV without clearance from both parents, and prohibited any reading material that did not come from the local religious bookstore. Even in high school, the girls were never allowed to wear make-up or talk about boys. Sexual topics were seen as filthy and disgusting. Arlene's brother, who was several years older and idolized by her parents, began molesting her when she was four. Because of the climate of the home, Arlene could not risk telling anyone for fear of punishment and disbelief. In working with Arlene, it became necessary to focus not only on the responsibility of her brother but also on the accountability of her parents. Her parents had been unable to recognize what was happening under their noses in the home environment they had created.

It is not always that parents or significant others know what is going on and fail to act. Often, molestations are occurring but parents or significant adults fail to read the warning signs.

Laura, a young woman in our support group, recalls begging her grandmother not to leave her alone with her grandfather. He would repeatedly molest her when the grandmother left the home. Since Laura was very young when this began, and had been threatened by her grandfather if she told, she could not understand how her grandmother could continue to ignore her obvious cries for help.

It is for this lack of knowledge that they hold a measure of accountability. (For warning signs in children see chart on page 65). Various other people, such as sisters, brothers, aunts, and family friends, can be seen by the victims as co-contributors. And they may indeed hold a measure of responsibility depending on the individual cases.

Some of you have had a child who was molested by a person outside of the family, or you may have been molested as a child by a teacher, a friend of the family, or by a babysitter. Because children in these situations often feel their parents should have known and should have protected them, it is important that you own a measure of responsibility. It is not that you participated, condoned, or even had specific knowledge of what was taking place. But you should have known your child well enough to have been able to read the signs in their behavior and to take action to stop the abuse in the early phases.

However, if you are a parent whose child was molested, do not let the guilt overcome you. This, too, can be destructive. As a parent, I realize the awesome responsibility I have to my two little girls, and yet, knowing as much as I know, educating them as well as I have, there are no guarantees that I can protect them from the sin that another person chooses to commit against them. As I am learning, "all things work together for good to those who love God, to those who are the called according to His purpose" (Rom. 8:28). I sincerely believe that nothing happens in our lives or in the lives of our children that our God is not able to redeem.

Minimizing Your Experience
We have discussed how the victim's guilt over the incident and her fear of losing a valued relationship often prevents her from establishing responsibility. There is one other significant issue—the victim's attempt to minimize the act or intent of the aggressor. By minimizing, or denying, the victim removes the significance of the event to free herself and her perpetrator. This is especially common in sibling incest where the ages of the children are relatively close. Most victims who have been molested by older brothers write off their experience to "exploration" or "inquisitiveness." I believe, as do many experts in child development, that experimentation is a normal part of growing up. It is when a child feels they are being acted upon, used, or powerless that the experimentation ceases. When the child no longer has a choice because of physical, psychological, or emotional coercion, the experimentation has turned into an act of molestation.

Warning Signs in Children

Symptoms *	*Observable Behavior*
1. Fear of specific persons or situations/strangers	Child verbally declares she doesn't want to go to "grampa's house" or shies away when around that person, or around strangers.
2. Nightmares	Usually has dreams of "helplessness"–trying to run away but being caught.
3. Withdrawl (Social or emotional)	Stays in room; isolates self; is sullen; "Just leave me alone."
4. Bed wetting/change in sleep patterns	Says, "Mom, I had an accident," or, "I can't sleep."
5. Personality change	Outgoing child who was a leader type becomes withdrawn; change in school performance.
6. Loss of appetite; increase in physiological complaints	"I'm not hungry." "My tummy hurts."
7. Unprovoked crying spells	Bursts into tears when significant parent goes on routine errands and leaves child, i.e., "Please, Mommy, don't leave me!"

Symptoms *	*Observable Behavior*
8. Clinging to significant adult	Stays in close proximity—needs more physical touching.
9. Excessive washing/baths	Talks of being dirty, feels dirty.
10. Poor self-image/low self-esteem	Increases negative self-incrimination—"I'm no good;" "I can't do anything right;" etc.
11. Changes in type of fantasy play	Expresses extreme victimization/violence in play
12. Fear of being alone	"Please, Mommy, stay with me. Don't turn out the light."
13. Refusal to go to school	Expresses dislike: doesn't want to go see friends. "I just want to stay home."
14. Running away	Retreats to "safe" family. "I don't like it here."
15. Attempt to control environment/fear of unknown	Exhibits need for excessive control; often becomes extremely anxious over unknown aspects of life. "What if our house catches on fire?" or, "Mommy, I'm afraid."

16. Early sexual
     precociousness

Practices excessive master-
bation; uses sexually ex-
plicit words and gestures
inappropriate for age.

*One or even two of these symptoms are not indicative of sexual abuse. A combination of several (four or more) might indicate a need for parental concern.

Audrey was a case in point. She came to our group feeling a bit out of place. She had said to me over the phone, "I sure have all the symptoms you talk about but I just don't see how that one little incident with my brother could have caused all this. We were just kids, and you know how kids experiment. How could he have known any better? He was only eight years old and I was five. He was just a kid himself." In therapy, we discussed how the first incident may have genuinely been child experimentation, but as Audrey shared other incidents it became clear that more was involved. Finally she said, "It really only started to bother me when he tied me down and brought friends over after school. By that time, I'd really gotten scared and was afraid to tell my parents for fear of punishment." We established in Audrey's case that her brother and she were both victims of their parents' inability to communicate and demonstrate love and thus her parents held a measure of responsibility. This in no way minimized her brother's accountability for his action. It merely helped to shed light on the circumstances that contributed to the family dysfunction.

Again, let me reiterate that the goal of establishing responsibility is not to push blame in all directions in order to give the victim a "blank slate." The primary function is to place responsibility where it belongs. Once the victim establishes the responsibility of the aggressor and any co-contributors in past traumatic incidents, she can go on to realistically assume responsibility for today, for her own life, without centering today's blames and responsibilities in and on the past. Many times the victims are so overburdened by assuming the false guilt and responsibility of others that they are unable to take on the responsibility that *is* rightfully their own. Balance of responsibility is a vital component in the future wholeness of the victim and the restoration of the family.

Scriptural Foundation for Accountability

What, if anything, does the Scripture have to say about accountability? We find many instances in both the Old and the New Testaments about accountability: David and Bathsheba, Ananias and Sapphira, Nebuchadnezzar, and the woman at the well. All these people were brought to account for their sin in one way or another. David was forgiven by God for adultery and murder, but he still faced the consequences of his sin. Ananias and Sapphira were judged for lying to the Holy Spirit and instantaneously stricken dead. Nebuchadnezzar experienced temporary insanity for arrogance and pride but was later restored to health. Finally the woman at the well was jolted into reality when Jesus confronted her about her past five husbands and her present living arrangement with a man who was not her husband.

The Old Testament story of Achan in Joshua 7 has a tremendous message particularly applicable to the establishment of responsibility. Joshua assumed the leadership of the Israelites at the death of Moses. In the first chapter of Joshua he was commanded to "be strong and of good courage" and to go forth and possess the land which God had promised to the people. In chapters 2 and 3, we see the miraculous ways God went before His people by preserving the two spies and by parting the Jordan River. In chapter 4, God called the nation to memorialize and worship Him for what had taken place. In chapter 5, the Lord called the nation to sanctify itself through the symbolic act of circumcision. Then the people began to eat of the good of the land and Joshua came face to face with God.

In the detailed account in chapter 6 of the fall of Jericho, God demonstrated His mighty power through those who were obedient to His Word. As is so common after a great victory, Israel fell into sin. We read in Joshua 7:1:

> But the children of Israel committed a trespass regarding the accursed things, for Achan the son of Carmi, the son of Zabdi, the son of Zerah, of the tribe of Judah, took of the accursed things; so the anger of the LORD burned against the children of Israel.

Joshua was not aware of Achan's activity when he sent men to survey the enemies at Ai. In verse 3 we find that the men returned to Joshua and said, "Do not let all the people go up, but let about two or three thousand men go up and attack Ai. Do not weary all the people there, for the people of Ai are few." As a result of failing to consult God and because of the secret sin of Achan, Israel suffered such a great defeat that their "hearts . . . melted . . . like water" (7:5 NIV). Joshua responded by tearing his clothes and falling on his face, and in verses 7 through 9 he lamented their predicament before God.

I love verse 10! I paraphrase it this way: "And the Lord said unto Joshua, 'Get up and do something! Why are you lying on your face?'" The Lord disclosed to Joshua that someone in the camp had sinned and that hidden sin had caused the defeat at Ai. God further warned the Israelites that until the sin was dealt with they could not stand before their enemies. He instructed Joshua to find the one who had transgressed and to burn that man with all his possessions. When Joshua found that Achan was guilty, he invited him to confess his sin. In verses 20 and 21, Achan reveals that he had taken a garment, money, and a wedge of gold and hidden them underneath his tent. Joshua commanded messengers to retrieve the stolen

69

items and they were laid out before the people and the Lord. In verses 24-26 we see Achan, his family and all his possessions brought to the Valley of Achor where he and his family were stoned to death and then burned and thus brought to accountability for their sin.

Before we go on, let's see what similarities exist between this story and the life of the incest victim. The victim is much like Israel in this account. The perpetrator has taken from the victim some valued possession and he hides his sin, just as Achan stole forbidden articles and hid his sin. The victim suffers defeat in her life due to the sin committed against her just as Israel suffered defeat at Ai due to Achan's sin. It was not until Achan was faced, confronted, and held accountable for his sin that Israel could go on to be victorious in battle once more. I believe the victim must face the reality of her offender's sin against her, confront if appropriate, and hold him accountable for his actions. This does not mean that we as victims take revenge, but it does mean we charge to the offender's account the sin and injustices he inflicted upon us. We ultimately leave the judgment of the sin to God. However, accountability may require that legal action be taken. This should not be viewed by Christians as a desire for revenge. It is simply allowing natural consequences to follow a sinful act. As mentioned earlier, God demonstrated this in His relationship with David. David was forgiven but he was allowed to suffer the consequences of his sin. Because David had despised the commandment of the Lord, the sword would never depart from his household and he would suffer the loss of the infant son born as a result of his sin (2 Sam. 12:9-14).

You may ask why establishing responsibility or accountability is so important for the victim. One summer day I turned to the book of Hosea for my devotions. Hosea was a prophet whom I have always admired. He was called to live out (on a daily basis) the analogy of adulterous Israel. In chapter 2 we read of God's love for His unfaithful people. Verses 14 and 15 came alive to me that morning!

> Therefore, behold, I will allure her,/ Will bring her into the wilderness,/ And speak comfort to her./ I will give her her vineyards from there,/ And the *Valley of Achor as a door of hope;*/ She shall sing there,/ As in the days of her youth,/ As in the day when she came up from the land of Egypt (emphasis mine).

The Holy Spirit began to teach me how vital these verses are for victims. In my own life, He had to take me through that wilderness period. I was bearing no fruit and my life was desolate in many areas. During this time I became aware of the symptoms in my life. Then the Holy Spirit began speaking tenderly to me and urging me to seek counseling.

Soon I began to see the fruit of that counseling even though it was a very painful time. The Valley of Achor became a "door of hope" to me in two very distinct ways. In Hebrew *achor* means trouble. How many times God uses the Valley of Trouble in our lives to bring us to a point of hope! At that time, I had no idea I would be sharing as I am today with thousands of victims. The second significance Achor has is shown in the story of Achan in Joshua 7; it was the valley of accountability in Achan's life. God showed me how essential this concept was in freeing me from bondage. I had to establish the accountability of my parents and release myself from false guilt. This issue of accountability was the first crucial step in being able to proceed with healing. After the Valley of Achor became my door of hope, I began to sing as I had in my youth, prior to the molestation. I was in the process of being freed from the bondage of Egypt.

Restoration As a Goal

As I reflected on these verses for several days, the Holy Spirit continued to inspire me. It was as if He said, "Jan, this is what you must share. I desire to do a healing work with my people. They are experiencing a desolation in their lives and I am using this place to begin the healing. I want them to bear fruit in the place of desolation but there is work to be done before that happens."

I was reminded of the verses in Ezekiel 36:34-36 in which the Lord says,

> The desolate land shall be tilled instead of lying desolate in the sight of all who pass by. So they will say, "This land that was desolate has become like the garden of Eden; . . . Then the nations which are left all around you shall know that I, the LORD, have rebuilt the ruined places and planted what was desolate. I, the LORD, have spoken it, and I will do it."

What a promise for victims! Notice, though, the use of the tilling process. It is not an easy one. In fact, it is very painful. Picture a large piece of desert land that has been parched by the sun. Nothing is growing there; it is useless. The soil has become hardened; it is cracking in areas. It cannot be dug up without obtaining special equipment because of its condition. The tilling process is an uprooting and upturning of the soil. It takes time. Even after the soil has been tilled and the seed planted, it will take time for the crop to appear.

It is just like that in the victim's life. She has areas of desolation. God requires an uprooting of the past that is very painful. He chooses often to use those who are specialized in the area of victimization as His tools in the tilling procedure. He begins to plant seeds in the former desolation and one day the garden will emerge. The vineyards bearing fruit will be visible to all and the heathen will give glory to God. For only He can take the desolation in a life and cause it to bear much fruit. The issue of accountability is the gateway for the victim to allow God to begin the planting of seeds. I believe the Holy Spirit used that passage in Hosea to show me how important it is for victims to take their offenders to the valley of account-ability. I have watched the process of healing in many women and have seen how vital this step of establishing responsibility is. It is the pathway to recovery.

I think of Lydia, a pastor's wife in her late forties. Lydia had trouble establishing her father's responsibility for the molestation. Because she was fourteen when it happened, she thought she should have been able to control him. She even admitted at times she enjoyed his attention. After several weeks of discussing the responsibility issue in the group, Lydia an-nounced to other members, "When Jan first mentioned this area, I was not receptive. I thought I was the only one to whom this didn't apply. During these past few weeks, I finally real-ized my dad *was* responsible for his actions. Since I began holding him accountable, I have sensed a new freedom and feel like there's hope for me." It was amazing to watch Lydia's progress over the next six months. By releasing herself and taking her offender to the valley of accountability, she allowed God to begin planting the seeds of truth in her life. She has been able to have a deeper, more intimate relationship with God and others as a result. She has also been able to share her experience with other women in her church and offer them hope for healing.

We have seen in this chapter what inhibits the victim from establishing responsibility: false guilt, fear of loss of valued relationships, and minimizing the significance of the act or intent of the aggressor. We have seen how God uses the establishment of responsibility and accountability in the lives of His people.

If you have been victimized, realize the "valley of account-ability" is your "door of hope." As you are able to establish the responsibility of your offenders, the door that has held you captive for years will begin to crack open ever so slightly. It is an opening to your freedom and your fruitfulness. The Holy

Spirit promises to "walk alongside" and is offering you hope and encouragement as you choose to walk through. Don't lose heart, your Eden lies ahead.

PRACTICAL INSIGHTS

1. Make a list of the ways in which you have held yourself accountable for the traumatic injury you experienced. If you were a victim of abuse as a child, find a picture of yourself at the age you first remember the abuse. As you look at that picture, ask yourself the following questions:

    a. Could I *really* have been responsible for what happened at this age?

    b. How did the child in the picture feel about what was occurring?

    c. Can you as an adult begin to release that child of the responsibility?
    If you are experiencing a deep emotional wound as an adult, examine the appropriateness of the accountability you have assumed and that which you've assigned to the offender. Make any adjustments necessary.

2. Read 2 Samuel 13:1-19. Notice the vulnerability of Tamar and the extreme rejection and guilt she experienced. Now read verses 20-39. There was no doubt in Absalom's mind where the accountability lay. (This does not endorse Absolom's actions, but merely points out his understanding of the accountability in this case.)

3. Memorize Isaiah 54:4-5.

CHAPTER 6

Step V:

Trace Behavioral Difficulties and Symptoms

Pastor and author Robert Schuller has made an interesting statement which particularly relates to this chapter. He says we must do three things with the problem areas in our lives: "Face them, trace them, and erase them." In this chapter we are going to focus on the latter two. What does it mean to trace the problem areas in our lives? It means we begin to look at the current patterns in our lives, particularly those that involve our interpersonal relationships, and identify the undesirable characteristics that predominate in our relating with others. After we identify those behavior patterns, we "trace" them back to when and where they originated in our lives. After we have traced them back to the root, we set about by a disciplined approach to "erase" those unhealthy and damaging patterns, replacing them with healthier ones.

Let me share a personal experience. Two years into our marriage, I found myself being extremely critical with my husband, Don. Whatever Don did, I would unknowingly find something wrong with it. He would lovingly dress my daughter in the morning and I would greet him by saying, "Why did you put *that* outfit on her? It's too cold outside for her to be in that." He would clear the breakfast dishes and I would respond critically, "Please don't put them on *that* counter. They belong over here." After going into the bathroom and finding it less than perfect, I would attack, "Can't you ever clean up the bathroom after you shower? You *never* pick up after yourself." As Don grew weary of the barrage of criticisms, I realized how miserable I was making him. And I felt miserable as well.

What to Look For

In the midst of therapy, my therapist encouraged me to trace the undesirable patterns in my life. One of the first ones I looked at was that of being overly critical. Where had that come from? To some extent patterns of communication, habits, mannerisms, gestures and personal idiosyncracies are rooted in the family background. These can be positive or negative characteristics which we carry into our marriage. Then we spend a lifetime with a mate trying to adjust to what they did or did not learn from their family of origin. Your spouse may squeeze the toothpaste tube in the middle, you religiously squeeze from the bottom. His clothes drawers are meticulously kept, yours look like a disaster area. Because modeling is so important in how children learn, we have come to realize that it is often not what children are told by their parents that impact them, but what they are shown.

In my home my stepdad was extremely critical. As a child, I may have done nine things right and one thing wrong but Dad always focused on that one wrong thing. Dinnertime in our home was usually an unpleasant experience. Dad would come home from work and we would eat promptly at 5:30 every evening. He would spend most of the dinner hour complaining about coworkers, ridiculing my mother, griping at us kids, or re-creating a scene at the office in which he had told someone off that day.

I never realized this had an effect on me until after I married. Don, Heather, and I were sitting eating dinner one evening. Four-year-old Heather was talking away, asking questions. Don and I were shoveling our food in without a word. Suddenly I realized we were not utilizing this important time to involve ourselves in pleasant conversation. As Don and I talked about it later that evening, we began tracing our patterns. Don came from a family of seven children, four boys and three girls. It was important in his home to eat fast to make sure he got "his fair share." I realized then that as a teenager I developed the art of gulping down my food so I could leave the table. The environment at the table had become so uncomfortable that I had subconsciously developed a pattern of eating that would remove me from the "pain."

As my husband and I talked it over that evening we decided to make a conscious effort toward making dinnertime a fun time for our children. We have developed some new conversational patterns and our little girl Heather has even made up some fun table games we play as a family.

It is important to note here that not all behavioral difficulties and symptoms are derived directly from the molestation experience. As we have noted before, there usually exist some dysfunctional patterns in the family prior to the incest. It is from these patterns that the incest flows. Most research tends to support this hypothesis. It is this very phenomenon that contributes to incest being carried from one generation to the next. The dysfunctional patterns of communication, the degree to which the family is a "closed system," and the family's inability to resolve conflicts in a healthy way are all contributory factors that either allow for or reduce dysfunction in the following generation.[1]

How Is Tracing Done?

What does tracing involve? It requires that you identify present patterns of behavior that are contributing to difficulties in your relationships in order to trace them back to their origin.

Picture this process as discovering a "short" in an electrical circuit. The "short" may be causing your living room lamp to flicker or go out unpredictably. You must examine the parts of the lamp carefully to determine the source of the short and then take measures to replace the dysfunctional part or parts. So it is in our relationships. We must look at different areas of life that are not functioning at their fullest potential and trace these back to the source. We then set about to replace these dysfunctional patterns with newer, healthy ones. It is essential that we depend upon the Holy Spirit for His direction and guidance in this area. The Scripture says in John 16:13 that the Holy Spirit's job is to "guide [us] into all truth." This truth involves more than just correct biblical theology. The Holy Spirit indwells us and sheds light into the areas of darkness in our life. Through His enabling, we are empowered to make changes. As I have gone to the Lord regarding the patterns in my own life that are not pleasing to Him and are unhealthy toward others, He has been faithful to expose them and to help me make changes.

Communication is often a problem for one who has been victimized. If you come from a family where communication was unclear or minimal, you will find yourself communicating in those same ways. If you come from a family where communication was superficial, you will have difficulty expressing your deep feelings and intimate thoughts.

Being a perfectionist is another behavioral symptom that may need adjustment. It often stems from a critical parent who was impossible to please. As adults we may find ourselves playing out the same role with our children that our parents played with us. Eating habits, money-spending, manipulation, rebelliousness to authority, and psychosomatic disorders all may stem from patterns developed in childhood. It is necessary to note that this tracing process often needs to be done with the assistance of a trained professional. During my therapy I looked at several of these patterns, learned how I could begin making some changes, and set about to do so. Since I have been out of therapy, the Lord continues to show me areas that need to be "faced, traced and erased." I attempt to trace these back to their origin and set a course for change.

Why Is This Necessary?

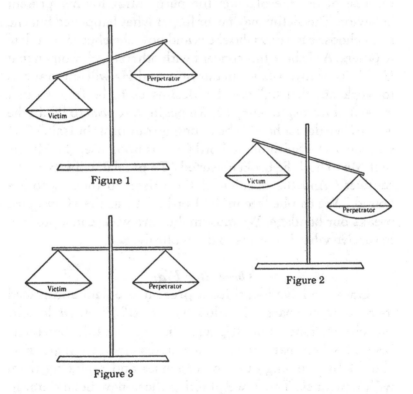

Figure 1

Figure 2

Figure 3

My therapist used an excellent illustration. He said, "Picture a scale. Often when victims come into therapy they are carrying the *total* weight of responsibility for all that has happened" (Figure 1). Through the therapy process we begin to shift the weight so that the perpetrator assumes the responsibility for what he has done (Figure 2). The goal of therapy is to establish a balance. The perpetrator is accountable for his part in the past victimization and the victim remains innocent. It is important to distinguish that the adult victim must begin to take responsibility for herself and her choices in the present and the future (Figure 3). It is no longer appropriate to spend the rest of her life blaming the perpetrator for her present behavior. The victim may never forget what happened but she must choose each day who she is and how she chooses to relate to others. As I share this concept with others, I tell women that God calls us to a balance in our lives and He will empower us to work out that balance. He desires us to be free, so that instead of *reacting* to our *past*, we begin to *respond* to life in the *present*. We do not have to be bound by our past. In Isaiah 61:1 we read, "The Spirit of the Lord GOD is upon Me, . . . /He has sent Me to heal the brokenhearted,/ To proclaim liberty to the captives,/ And the opening of the prison to those who are bound." We can be free in the Lord Jesus as the Holy Spirit breaks our bondage. We must make sure we are in a position to receive what He wants to do in our lives.

Three-Step Plan

Once we have identified a present problem and traced its roots to our past, what do we do next? First, we look at the circumstance that triggers the undesirable behavior. Second, when that circumstance arises again we make new choices by avoiding our old responses and replacing them with new ones. Third, we practice these new behaviors. In all of these we need the discernment, wisdom, and strength of the Holy Spirit. As you well know, it is not easy to change patterns that have taken a lifetime to form. It might help to share the following experience. Nancy, a pastor's wife, had been victimized by her stepfather as a young child. She was excessively overweight and although she had tried numerous diets and even considered surgery, she could not lose weight consistently over a period of time. As we looked at her eating patterns, we saw a significant link between her past and present behaviors. Nancy often overate when she was feeling depressed. The depression usually centered around her husband's frequent speaking engagements that took him out of town. Nancy would promise her husband that she would make a considerable effort to lose weight while he was gone, but she often gained weight.

As we traced this pattern in her life, she became aware that she never had an eating problem until her late teens, after her mother died. Then she developed binges that went on for days. For the first time Nancy realized that the fear of losing her husband was a major contributor to her unhealthy eating habits. She set about to change her behavior with God's help. When her husband had an upcoming trip, she would plan activities with the children that would keep her from sitting around the house feeling depressed. She would take a supportive friend along when she did the grocery shopping so she would make wise decisions and not buy cakes, cookies, and candies. She did not make promises to her husband any more concerning her weight, but began to value herself as she was, even though she was 150 pounds overweight. As she employed these steps, Nancy was amazed at the progress she made. There were times that she slipped back into her old patterns, but she has been able to control her eating and has lost a significant amount of weight.

God's Perspective

The erasing of habitual patterns is no easy job. It takes consistency, discipline and strength. I am reminded of a verse in Philippians 2:13 which says: "It is God who works in you both to will and to do for His good pleasure." I am so glad it doesn't totally depend on me!

Remember, tracing is a tool used to find the origin of faulty behavior patterns, not a tool to excuse or justify our conduct. The primary objective is to take that information and begin to map out a plan of action toward change. As I thought about this tool I wondered about its relevance in Scripture. Many times in the Old Testament we are warned not to be like our fathers who failed to obey God's commands: "And do not be like your fathers and your brethren. . . . Now do not be stiff-necked, as your fathers were" (2 Chron. 30:7-8).

God's Word declares that we carry patterns from one generation to the next as evidenced in Exodus 34:6-7. In the story of Eli and Samuel (1 Samuel 1-3), Eli failed "to restrain" his sons and as a result God pronounced judgment on Eli's house. Samuel was used, even as a child, to deliver the message of judgment to Eli. Although Samuel was also a prophet ordained by God, he, too, failed to learn the negative lesson exemplified in Eli's life. In 1 Samuel 8:1-3 we read that Samuel appointed his sons as judges over Israel but "his sons did not walk in his ways; they turned aside after dishonest gain, took bribes, and perverted justice." I wonder what would have happened if Samuel in his early adulthood had identified and traced some faulty patterns in his life. Would this have altered the way he raised his children? Since Eli was his primary model, Samuel was no doubt influenced by Eli's parenting techniques.

God grants us immeasurable grace in this life but it is my desire to "break the bands" that hold me in bondage, whether they are derived from my past or are a product of the present. There's a beautiful verse in Ezra 9:9 that clearly states God's purpose in our lives: "For we were slaves. Yet our God did not forsake us in our bondage; but He extended mercy to us . . . to revive us, to repair the house of our God, to rebuild its ruins, and to give us a wall in Judah and Jerusalem."

As the Holy Spirit led me to that verse, He showed me the significance of it for today. We are the temple of our God and it is His desire to restore the ruins in our lives. He wants to build us up in spite of the destruction we have carried with us from the battles of life. As Nehemiah learned when he rebuilt the wall in Jerusalem, it is no easy task, but one that we undertake knowing that God will oversee the project. I pray you will be encouraged to trace the ruins of your past, and today begin to build up your wall to the glory of God.

PRACTICAL INSIGHTS

1. Identify a current problem in your life that you wish to change. Ask the Holy Spirit to give you an awareness about the problem and to empower you to make changes. Examine the conditions under which you're most susceptible to this behavior occurring. Devise a detailed plan to avert this behavior the next time it arises, i.e., pray, go for a walk, bite your tongue, etc. Focus on this one area for at least two weeks and then evaluate if the plan is working or whether adjustments are needed to make it more effective.

2. Read Romans 6:4-22. Often what we so desperately cling to interferes with experiencing an intimate relationship with our Savior.

3. Memorize Philippians 2:13.

CHAPTER 7

Step VI:

Observe Others and Educate Yourself

L ast night was not unlike several other nights I have experienced over the last two years, and yet it was a unique and memorable evening. Eight of us gathered in what had come to be a very familiar room. It was our tenth and final session as a group who had gathered for a common purpose. As I sat there looking around I remembered how each person had entered ten weeks previously. Some were anxious, some withdrawn, some nervous, some reluctant—but all were there, I believe, to keep a divine appointment. I remembered how we went around the group, said our names, shared a little bit about our background, and expressed the goals we hoped to achieve. As I looked into the faces of those women again last night, my eyes welled up with tears because of the goodness of God. No one but God could take these women who had experienced the traumatic ordeal of incestuous relationships, place them in this environment for ten weeks, and develop a mutual bond of love in the midst of deep, personal pain.

When I asked them to share whether they would be continuing in the group or moving on, I felt the emotions of joy and sadness simultaneously. There was joy especially for Sandy who after being through two ten-week sessions had made such progress. She had successfully confronted her perpetrator and her family was taking steps toward restoration. But I felt sadness that Sandy was moving on. She would no longer be a part of this special group of women, at least in the physical sense. As Sandy expressed to each member how they had contributed to her in a personal way, sharing from her heart, I sensed the deep bond created through vulnerability during the previous weeks. As the group shared with Sandy, the theme reflected by all was essentially, "Thank you for allowing me to see you, your weaknesses, your failures, your past, your hopes, your goals, your pursuits." And Sandy seemed to be saying, "Thank you for accepting me for who I am and for challenging me to move forward and be the best that I can be to the glory of God." How merciful our God is to take the devastation and desolation of a life and begin a fruitful work of healing.

The Importance of Others

This sixth step, observing others and educating ourselves, may seem inconsequential; however, a turning point is in process. Up to this point we have focused primarily within. It is through this step that we begin to direct our focus outside ourselves. Although we have not completed the work that needs to be done within, we attempt to involve others in the process of healing and affect others by our healing. It is at this point that we receive and gain the benefits of being altruistic. We will discuss this more in a later chapter.

Why is it necessary to involve others in our healing process? In psychological terms, it is known as the therapeutic factor of universality. Simply stated, it means we, as hurting individuals, realize we are not unique or alone by encountering others who have gone through what we have experienced. As I speak in various parts of the country, sharing my story and the steps to healing, women always come to me afterward and say, "I knew I was not the only one who had ever been molested, but until hearing you today, I never knew anyone else had the same feelings and needs that I have." I cannot explain to you why this is such an important factor in the healing process, but I do know it has been supported by research done by Lieberman & Borman in 1979[1] and is demonstrated as one of the key elements in our support groups.

The Scripture seems to confirm this principle throughout the Old and New Testaments. Jesus is described in Isaiah 53:4 as the one who has "borne our griefs and carried our sorrows," and in Hebrews 4:15 we are told: "We do not have a High Priest who cannot sympathize with our weaknesses, but was in all points tempted as we are, yet without sin."

When we experience any type of loss, we find great comfort just being in the presence of someone else who has been where we are. This is why we encourage any type of victim to involve herself with others who have had a similar experience. It is this element of universality that motivates us to read certain books, watch particular TV shows, and attend numerous seminars. We have an innate need to say, "I am not alone in this."

Observing others has another positive effect. It allows us to gain insight into dealing with our specific situation. We have found in our groups that the women enter the group at different levels. Each has had a common experience and similar symptoms and feelings, but each has made progress in different areas and has learned to cope in unique ways. We encourage the women to share the ways in which they have coped, are coping, and hope to cope in the future.

Support Groups

Often we encounter resistance from people concerned over the emergence of the specialized support groups. They express fear that it may end up being a place where people get together and wallow in self-pity and defeat. We have found it to be quite the contrary. It is a place where a woman can come and be herself, let down all the masks that she wears during the week, and just cry, if that is what she needs to do. It is a place of hope, challenge, and encouragement. The direction and theme of the support group is very much the responsibility of its leaders. We as facilitators need to provide the guidelines, framework, and theme for the group, yet be flexible enough to realize it is *their* group designed for *their* healing, not a personal platform for leadership. Observing others allows us to see ourselves in a realistic light. It also provides us the opportunity to make changes where necessary. It is often through an educational process that change occurs.

Educate Yourself

I encourage the women I work with to educate themselves about the topic of incest: Read books and articles; listen to speakers, talk shows, and radio interviews. It is unfortunate that there is not much of this being done within the Christian community. Nevertheless, I challenge the women to read books and articles that are available in the Christian market on related topics such as self-esteem, understanding our emotions, and inner healing. The emphasis is directed toward a person's taking action on behalf of herself. At the time I was going through therapy, there were no support groups available so I began reading everything I could get my hands on. The understanding that came, even through some secular material, began to transform my thinking. After completing therapy, I attended a church seminar conducted by Dr. Betty Coble Lawther, our director of women's ministries. Betty's seminar, "Woman, Aware and Choosing," deals with self-esteem and the marriage relationship. Her concepts on self-esteem were instrumental in changing my life, and we will look at them in greater detail in chapter 10, the chapter on rebuilding our self-image.

We also use the support group environment as a place of education. We share well-researched information from an objective standpoint and allow the women to share from a subjective view. Although it is not always feasible, a great deal of hope is instilled in the women if a "recovered" victim is involved in the group. I am careful to put the word recovered in quotations, since it is my basic belief that I will always be in the process of recovery. As I share with women, I tell them that because of God's grace I am no longer bound by my past, but I fully believe I will always be in the healing process. God continues to use the support group as a tool of growth in my life as well. It is beneficial to the women that I have known a measure of their pain, yet have been able to overcome many of the symptoms and destructive patterns that usually encompass a victim. Observing others and educating ourselves provides a frame of reference, a source of identification, and an environment of acceptance. In this environment a woman can learn more about herself and her relationships and has a place to begin to incorporate and test new attitudes, behaviors, and beliefs.

Many victims have faulty belief systems that need to be challenged. They have distorted perceptions of God, of others, and of themselves. The support group provides relationships that can contradict some of these negative assumptions. We address these issues regularly by asking:

- What are some of your basic assumptions about yourself?
- Do you feel unlovable?
- Are you powerless?
- What are some of your assumptions about God?
- Do you believe God is watching you carefully so that when you mess up He can immediately zap you?
- Is God trustworthy?
- What do you believe to be true of others? Are you

suspicious of their motives? Do you mistrust their friendships? Are they out to get what they can from you? Do they leave as soon as you get close?

The women often find they share some of these negative assumptions. We attempt to challenge these on several levels. *First*, we challenge them verbally through the use of Scripture that invalidates their misconceptions. *Second*, others within the group share personal experiences that invalidate their assumptions. *Third*, in a very subtle way, the existence of the group itself denies the maintenance of many of these beliefs.

Observe Others

Brenda, who has been in three of our groups, is an illustration of a person who has a faulty belief system that needs to be challenged. Brenda was molested from age three to her teens by several males within her family. Her whole life had been a series of victimizations. Because of this, she developed an intricate system of defenses, negative assumptions and coping mechanisms in order to survive.

Brenda had many negative assumptions. One which significantly changed since her support group involvement was her false assumption that she would immediately be rejected if she talked to anyone about her past. She even avoided the conscious recall of memories because she felt God would punish her for remembering such evil things.

We worked on several levels with Brenda. *First*, we shared God's total, unconditional acceptance of her as stated in His Word. *Second*, we were able to show her that other women in the group, although they disclosed events of their past, were not rejected by the group. *Third*, we provided Brenda the opportunity to share one-on-one with another group member at least one event from her past.

From these three levels, Brenda was able to come to the

cognitive conclusion that she could discuss her past and not face rejection. The group experience helped her to begin to change some interpersonal relationships outside the group as well. Brenda is slowly coming to the realization that God is not displeased with her, but is on her side urging her to release the poison that has affected her relationship with Him and with others.

As you have been reading, I hope you have been able to grasp the underlying goal of all that we have discussed thus far. *It is change.* We do not gather women together merely to educate them, have them share some similar past experiences and leave it at that. We are in this together as a means to effect change. We understand that each one is progressing at her individual rate and that we would negate what we are trying to accomplish if we tried to force members to fit a specific mold.

We have found, as have many others, that the support group environment provides the setting in which change can begin to occur. If you are a victim, I encourage you to find at least one other person who knows your inner pain because she has been there. If you are a pastor or church leader, why not step out and begin to meet the needs of your people? I will discuss in a later chapter the details and guidelines of starting support groups for victims.

In his book *Growing Strong in the Seasons of Life,* Chuck Swindoll writes, "Tucked away in a quiet corner of every life are wounds and scars. If they were not there, we would need no physician. Nor would we need one another."[2] We do need each other. Last night was one of those nights that confirmed our need to be connected to one another. Sandy would, no doubt, tell you it is worth it. Reach out!

PRACTICAL INSIGHTS

1.   Read at least one book that relates to your specific area of hurt, i.e., divorce, molestation, adultery, alcoholism.

(There is a suggested reading list in the appendix for victims of sexual abuse.) Jot down any new insight you receive and, based on that, implement at least one new way of thinking, feeling, or behaving as a result. Share your emotional hurt with a person who you feel will be supportive and accepting. Plan to get together with that person (or another victim) on a regular basis for support.

2. Read 1 Corinthians 12:12-26. You are a necessary part of the body of Christ. You can be assured that, even in the midst of working through your crisis, others besides yourself may benefit.

3. Memorize Hebrews 10:24-25.

CHAPTER 8

Step VII:

Confront the Aggressor

rom the victim's point of view, confronting the aggressor is one of the hardest of the ten steps. When I share this concept with women in my support groups, I get a myriad of responses: "I couldn't possibly do it." "I have done it before and it didn't work." "What good will that do?" Another common response is, "I'm a Christian. How can I confront this person when Christ teaches forgiveness?"

I have news for you: Confrontation is not unbiblical!

In this chapter, I will discuss:

- What is confrontation?
- Why is confrontation necessary?
- Who needs to be confronted?
- When should you confront?
- What should confrontation include?
- How can it be accomplished?
- Does confrontation always work?

Confrontation should not be undertaken on the basis of reading this book only. There are several individual factors that must be carefully examined with the help of a professional to determine whether confrontation is appropriate and in the best interest of the victim.

What Is Confrontation?

Before we discuss the whys of confrontation, let's examine what confrontation means and what it should accomplish. According to Webster's dictionary, confronting means to "bring face to face." Unfortunately, most of us picture a confrontation as a knock-down-drag-out fight, which can and often does include verbal abuse and physical violence. Keep in mind, however, that confrontation for our purposes means bringing face to face. If we are to bring issues face to face with another person, we must first of all check our motivation. What is the intent behind the confrontation? When women consult with me about a confrontation with the aggressor, we wrestle with this issue. I ask them what they want from this confrontation. Is it revenge? Recognition? Restoration? Reconciliation? It may be a combination of many things, but the underlying motivation should be reconciliation. Many victims assume that reconciliation means they must totally embrace the aggressor, discount what has happened and by no means express anger. This is not true. To have reconciliation as a goal means the victim desires harmony in the relationship and a settling or resolution of past issues.

Confrontation is not recommended for victims who are still minors or victims whose perpetrators are far-removed, having little or no contact, or victims who would put themselves at risk by confronting. There may come a time when, since the involved parties have become adults, these confrontations can take place, but it is solely an individual matter needing prayerful consideration.

When a victim does confront a perpetrator within the immediate or extended family, she must remember she is only accountable for herself. She must not assume responsibility for the aggressor's reaction or the future of the responsibility.

Why Is Confrontation Necessary?

As you recall, we talked in chapter five about the crucial step of establishing responsibility. Confrontation takes the establishment of responsibility one step further. It enables the victim to take the burden of responsibility and *place it* in the rightful hands of the aggressor and any co-contributors. Let me explain by way of example. As a mother, I have several regular household duties I perform. I have established responsibilities for my daughter also, such as picking up her toys before bedtime each evening. If I have established that as her responsibility, yet I continue to pick up her toys for her, it really has not become her responsibility. I must, at some point, place that responsibility in her hands and make her accountable for it. The same is true with being a victim. You may have given mental assent to the fact that the aggressor is responsible for what happened, but until you place that responsibility in his hands by confrontation, you are probably carrying some, if not all of the burden.

Confrontation, then, is the actual placing of responsibility in the hands of its rightful owners. *This may be done directly with the offender present or by role-playing in a therapeutic environment.* This enables the victim to unload a burden she has carried, which in reality was not hers to carry. She can unload the excess baggage and begin to be responsible for only what is hers.

As I mentioned earlier, confrontation—bringing issues face to face—is a biblical concept. Confrontation is clearly spoken about in both the Old and New Testaments. We have a beautiful example of confrontation and reconciliation in the life of King David in 2 Samuel 12:1-23. Look at it from the perspective of a confrontation. In chapter 11, King David commits adultery, gets Bathsheba pregnant, and in an attempt to cover his sin, cunningly arranges for Bathsheba's husband, Uriah, to meet an untimely death in battle. David assumes his sin is hidden; however, the Lord is fully aware and displeased with David's sin. In chapter 12 the Lord summons Nathan, the prophet, to go to David and confront him. There is no doubt that the Lord is also grieved over David's sin. Nathan uses a divinely inspired analogy to bring David's sin to light and in verses 7 through 9 Nathan openly and directly exposes the specifics of David's sin. God uses direct face-to-face confrontation to bring David to accountability. In verse 13, we see David's admission of sin and his response of repentance.

This story is a key to understanding the biblical perspective of confrontation. It brings issues face to face and has a goal of reconciliation. Some of you are no doubt saying, "Yes, but the Bible also says forgive others as Christ has forgiven you. Why shouldn't I just forgive and forget without going through the painful process of confrontation?" It simply does not work. I tried this forgive-and-forget policy for nearly twenty years. Finally I discovered that I merely camouflaged the anger, bitterness and resentment. While trying desperately to bury my traumatic past, I found it lived out in my daily life, masked as uncontrollable anger toward my toddler, critical resentment toward my husband, rebellion to authority, an uncertainty about God, and a personal deep sense of worthlessness. This portion of Scripture, and others, have convinced me that confrontation is a valuable biblical tool when used correctly. Matthew 18:15 says, "If your brother sins against you, go and tell him his fault between you and him alone. If he hears you, you have gained your brother."

In his book *Caring Enough to Confront*, David Augsburger writes, "Life without confrontation is directionless, aimless, passive. When unchallenged, human beings tend to drift, to wander or to stagnate."[1] When Jesus dealt with people, He constantly modeled confrontation as an effective means of motivation. He confronted the woman at the well about her immorality. He confronted the Pharisees about their deception. He confronted Peter about his denial. Jesus' goal was not to instill guilt but to help people face the reality of who they were and where they were headed if they failed to change. He faced them with the responsibility of their actions and challenged them to be different.

Confrontation may be used as a tool to benefit the offender. I have known of several men who have sexually abused their children, and they are so filled with guilt and remorse that it physically affects them. Their victims had chosen to allow the "secret" to remain intact when, in actuality, healing could have come to both the victim and the aggressor if confrontation had taken place. Julie found this to be true. For years Julie had kept silent about the incestuous relationship with her father. She bore the guilt and responsibility, not wanting to confront him because it didn't seem to be "the Christian thing to do." After being a part of the support group, she realized it was a necessary part of her emotional healing. As a result of her confrontation, her relationship with her mother, father and siblings was restored. Her father, who had been an alcoholic, chose to seek help for his various problems and the family began to pursue reconciliation actively among its members.

Confrontation is a means of breaking the incestuous pattern. Victims need to realize that confrontation forces the aggressor and significant others in his life to face his problem squarely. Too many victims who have chosen not to confront have indirectly contributed to the aggressor victimizing someone else, sometimes even the victim's own child. Ellen, a member in my first support group, had to come to grips with this issue. She is a devoted Christian, a wife, and the mother of three daughters. She had been molested by her father for several years and could identify with many of the victim's symptoms described earlier. She also observed that her oldest daughter, Karie, had some typical symptoms, including a fear of her grandfather. Ellen had sensitively asked her daughter if Grandpa had ever touched her. Karie replied that he had not but continued to exhibit fearfulness and withdrawal. Ellen prayed that the Lord would show her why Karie was experiencing these problems and how to help her. After being in the support group for several months Ellen realized she needed to confront her father. She lived near her parents and even worked part-time in the family business. The weekly contact became unbearable and she knew she must bring the issues into the open.

Ellen arranged the confrontation with her parents and had her therapist present. After Ellen shared some specific details and the goal of the confrontation, her father openly admitted his responsibility and, in addition, confessed the details of an encounter with Karie. Two years prior he had exposed himself and coerced Karie into touching his "private parts." Ellen was beside herself. Now it all made sense to her. She had been asking Karie the wrong question. Karie had answered truthfully: Grandpa had never touched her. Ellen realized the intense guilt little Karie must have felt for over two years. Karie didn't know the act of aggression wasn't her fault. Although devastated by this incident in her daughter's life, Ellen later said, "At least now I know, Jan. If I had not gone through this confrontation with my father, I might never have known the reason for my daughter's fears. At least now I can do for her what my mother never did for me."

As Exodus 34:6-7 indicates, the sins of the fathers are visited upon their children, and upon their children's children unto the third and fourth generations. Secular studies demonstrate this biblical truth as seen in a research paper done by Dr. Roland Summit entitled "Typical Characteristics of Father-Daughter Incest: A Guide for Investigation." Summit states:

A remarkable proportion of the mothers of abused children are themselves survivors of sexual abuse. Exact numbers are difficult to find. One treatment center for child abuse has found consistently that more than 80 percent of the mothers in the program have a background of sexual abuse. Some victims can trace sexual abuse to their mothers and even their grandmothers, making a legacy of four generations of sexual victimization.[2]

The pattern must be broken. It is clear from Ellen's story that Grandpa's problem was not merely some isolated incident years ago but that he carried the sin with him. Another thirty-five-year-old woman in one of my groups told me she hates to visit her parents' home back East because her father still exposes himself to her. He is seventy-nine years old.

Statistics also indicate that a very high percentage of women victims marry men who then victimize their children. That is tragic! Someone must be willing to stand up, confront the issue and put a stop to this destructive pattern.

It may not be a pleasant task. Confrontation sometimes results in some unpleasant natural consequences for the aggressors. The victim must be careful not to try to circumvent or feel responsible for such events. This will be discussed further in the next chapter.

Who Needs To Be Confronted?

The next critical issue of confrontation is: Who needs to be confronted? For most, it is obvious that the aggressor is the one who needs to be confronted. However, the co-contributors also need to be faced with their responsibility.

For years I directed all the responsibility, anger and hostility toward my stepfather. But when I was in my early twenties, a friend who knew what had happened commented, "You're really angry with your mother as well."

I vehemently disagreed, "I adored and admired my mother. She was a saint to put up with my stepfather all those years."

My friend's comment stuck in my head for years, though. Finally, in therapy I saw that he was right. I realized that my mother, too, was responsible for what had happened, and she needed to be confronted.

Mothers often indirectly encourage incestuous relationships. In her book *Betrayal of Innocence*, Susan Forward states that the mother, whom she refers to as "the silent partner," "is a participant whether she knows about the incest or not, though her participation is often characterized more by what she does *not* do than by what she does." I have worked with many women and children whose mothers, when confronted with the undeniable evidence of molestation within the family, could not face the reality and simply went into denial. I have found that frequently these mothers also were victimized as children. Because of their inability to deal with their own victimization, and their basic coping style of denial, these women find it too painful and guilt-producing to face the victimization of their child.

Additionally, mothers may find themselves intimidated by physical or emotional harm or financial insecurity, and therefore ignore the symptoms or the accusations of the victim. By remaining in the situation, the mother fosters the continuance of the incestuous relationship.

"The silent partner's general disenchantment—and resultant emotional neglect of her family—is subtle," writes Susan Forward.[3] I refer to this as emotional distancing. Through her indifference to her husband and lack of sensitivity toward her child, the mother sets the scene for incest.

At the base of every incestuous family there is a breakdown in the marital relationship. Communication skills between the marriage partners are poor and usually one mate dominates the other. Their sexual relationship may or may not be lacking. There is, however, a definite emotional chasm that alienates the male partner and causes him to search for some balance, often through a relationship with his daughters. There is, of course, the issue of the individual as well. Many aggressors were victims as children and as mentioned previously, mothers who marry aggressors often are victims, too. Further, an aggressor is usually characterized by low self-esteem and poor impulse control. He may present himself as a domineering man who is a rigid authoritarian and may be overly protective of his daughters. Or he may be a weak and passive man who constantly lives in the shadow of a domineering wife. It is important to realize that he is not a dirty old man lurking around street corners. He is usually a highly intelligent man and is often a pillar of the community. I have letters from victims all over the country whose perpetrators were highly respected men, including pastors, doctors, evangelists, policemen and other professionals.

Many victims paint similar pictures of their aggressors. Often the aggressor attempts to feel emotionally balanced through tyrannizing his children. Most authorities agree that the incestuous incident is in actuality not a sexual act, but rather an attempt at gaining control or feeling a sense of power. Both types of aggressors—the passive, weak aggressor who lives in the shadow of his wife and the domineering authoritarian—are no doubt products of their past.

Other people may be co-contributors or aggressors themselves. Brothers, cousins, uncles, aunts, grandfathers, grandmothers, or mothers' boyfriends may directly or indirectly contribute to the incestuous relationship. These people need to be held accountable as well. Carla, a woman in my support group, was molested by her uncle. She recalls her brother walking into the room on one occasion. Carla remembers with anger that he merely watched what was going on for a few seconds and quietly walked out of the room. In some ways, Carla was as angry with her brother as she was with her uncle.

When there has been sibling incest, most commonly that

of an older brother with his younger sister, it is important to focus not only on the aggressor, but on the whole family structure. In counseling these women, I often find that the parents have been extremely negligent in some areas of child rearing. Sometimes they fostered an attitude that women are nonpersons or at least are subordinate to men and may, therefore, be used. When the incestuous relationships have spanned an extended period of time, it is indicative of some emotional withdrawal by the parents. I try to help victims examine their family dynamics and begin to place responsibility, not only with their aggressor but also with the parents who have allowed the conditions to exist.

It is my firm belief that children give signals that indicate their lack of comfort in a relationship. Parents who invest themselves in the lives of their children can pick up on these signals. Parents who have withdrawn or lack sensitivity will fail to recognize them. It is often painful for victims to get in touch with their feelings toward their parents in this situation, but it is very necessary for the total healing of *all* the family members.

When Should You Confront?

The victim must identify the people in her life who must be confronted for their individual responsibilities. The "when" of the confrontation issue may be the most important. A premature confrontation may be very devastating and counterproductive. I often tell victims it is better to wait than to proceed before they are ready. Several ingredients should be present prior to any attempt at confrontation. *First*, the victim must feel a strength in her position. Too many victims have attempted a confrontation from a position of weakness, rather than a position of strength. The victim must *know* beyond a shadow of a doubt that she is totally innocent and devoid of any responsibility for the incident or incidents.

Many women struggle with this issue. Grace was a woman who could not release herself from responsibility. "I remember hating what was happening," she recalls, "but at the same time I liked it. It was the only closeness I ever felt as a child. In some ways, I can see I set myself up for it happening again and again." As I counseled Grace, I told her, "Your father perverted your God-given childlike need for love in an attempt to satisfy his own needs. As time went on, you continued to need appropriate love, yet each time, you were given a counterfeit. Grace, you never should have been placed in that kind of position. Your father is accountable for activating a response cycle within you that he had no business activating, and one that you had difficulty controlling from then on." It is of utmost importance that the victim acknowledge the complete accountability of the aggressor before confrontation is undertaken.

Second, she must do some preliminary work with her own self-esteem and gain assertiveness in her everyday life. In other words, she must show signs of confidence in herself, rather than reverting back to the victim role.

In my own case, this position of strength was developed through some tough decisions. I began to realize that every time I was about to see my stepfather at a family gathering, I became anxiety-stricken. I was short-tempered with my husband and had a feeling of being "out of control."

I had confronted my stepfather on two previous occasions in an attempt to reconcile and had been met with total denial and rejection. A third time I confronted him in anger. Neither of these approaches worked. Then I sought counsel from some very dear Christian friends. They recommended that I withdraw from my stepfather for an unspecified amount of time and essentially refuse to see him. At first I said, "There is no way I can do that. How will I explain this to my mother? What can I say to make her understand? This certainly can't be the Christian thing to do!"

Another respected spiritual leader gave me the same counsel. It confirmed in my mind that this was the best course of action. My first two attempts to confront my stepfather had been done from a position of weakness, not from one of strength. My friends made me realize that I was hoping and in a sense *asking* my stepfather to take responsibility for what he had done. I had gone to him as a pleading child, rather than as a knowing, adult woman. Then when I went to him in anger, I left no room for reconciliation and healing, and was, therefore, met with defensiveness. In each situation, I had given my stepfather the control, and now I had to take control of the situation myself. My friends shared with me that this choice was not only for myself, but for my husband and child who were being victimized by me due to my intense anxiety.

My husband supported my decision to call my mother. That phone call was very difficult but I had made my choice! As I spoke with my mother I told her I suffered from emotional stress every time I saw my stepfather and that I could no longer see him. Her immediate response was, "Why are you doing this now? What am I going to tell him? How long is this going to last?" I explained that I was making a choice for myself and my family. I had no idea how long this decision would last. It was a step toward resolving past issues. I told her I would be happy to explain my decision to him, although I knew she would not wish me to do so. I then expressed my desire to continue to have a relationship with her and allow her to visit whenever she wished. I offered to drive my daughter up to meet her at a local restaurant or to go to her home when my stepfather was not there. I gave her the opportunity to respond. I had made a decision and allowed her to make her own decisions based upon mine. The separation between my stepfather and me lasted one year with the exception of two brief encounters.

In retrospect I can see the importance of that step. It was as though I had been walking around for years with an open wound inflicted upon me by my stepfather. During brief periods of separation from him, the wound, although still present, did not ache as much. The anticipation of seeing him again and the actual face-to-face meeting ripped off the scab that had begun to form and poured salt into the wound. His rejection and denial only made the pain intensify. The separation allowed me time to gain strength and allowed the wound to begin healing from the inside out.

Separation was the first of three steps that were essential in leading to a confrontation. The second step was not as premeditated as the first, but the significance of it became very clear to me as time went on.

In the fall of the year, I enrolled in a woman's Bible study at our church that was using Verna Birkey's study guide *You Are Very Special*. We spent five months identifying who we were in God's eyes. Birkey's book pointed out Scripture after Scripture that showed me I was of value to God — I was chosen by Him and was His "special treasure." Although I had been a Christian nearly twenty years, this concept really hit home for the first time. I saw that, in order to love my husband and my child the way I wanted to, I had to begin to love myself. This revolutionized my thinking and my actions. I did not realize it at the time but God knew I needed a new self-image. Through His Word and through choices I made daily, my self-esteem improved. I actually began to like myself and could even accept a compliment graciously.

I began to take God at His word and accept His unconditional love for me. This initial step became my foundation, but it is a difficult process for a victim to initiate. I had *trusted* someone who was supposed to love and protect me. This trust had been betrayed and I was left devastated. I found it difficult initially to reach out to God because of my own questions about

God's trustworthiness. At times it became sheer discipline of mind that kept me hanging on to God's truth.

After our Bible study on self-worth, we elected to begin studying Myrna Alexander's book *Behold Your God*,[4] a study on the various attributes of God. The Lord knew I needed to reconstruct the image I had of myself but I also needed to restore a right image of God. Through this study of His Word, I saw how I had been in error about the person of God. I had transferred the characteristics of my human stepfather to my heavenly Father. It was no wonder that when I sinned I felt the Lord was going to zap me at any time! I saw every bad thing that happened in my life as a punishment from God. How many of us think of our God in these human terms? Yes, God in His grace knew I needed a new image of Him! As Paul says in Philippians 3:10, our goal should be to "know Him." Through the new images of myself and of God, I began to see the past and present circumstances of my life from a new perspective. Finally, I was able to understand that God did not direct the trauma of the past, but through His sovereignty and grace He could take that trauma, redeem it, and turn it into triumph.

The third step was also a very difficult one to take. Although I had made progress in the areas of my self-image and my image of God, I was still experiencing a great deal of depression. I seemed to become increasingly angry with my husband and often felt explosive anger toward my toddler. One spring day we made plans to go to the beach. While I was still in bed, my husband lovingly got our daughter up, dressed her, and began to feed her breakfast. I greeted my husband that morning by saying, "You gave her too much cereal." Throughout the day I continued to criticize everything he did. "Can't you help me load the car?" "Why are we parking so far away?" "Do you have to take her in the water *now*?" "Look at her, how could you let her get so sandy before lunch?" "Why

are you stopping here—I just want to get home!" At the end
of the day my dear husband felt like he had been through
World War II and lost! I was aware of how miserable it was
to be around me and yet I could not seem to change.

Often I listened to a Christian radio host counseling different women with various problems. Frequently, he recommended that the callers seek professional help with a Christian
specializing in their problem, or that they find a specialized
support group. A light clicked on for me. I knew I had reached
an impasse and that it was time to reach out for help. I followed
the radio host's advice and got a referral for a therapist who
specialized in the area of incest. Because our financial situation
was so limited, it was a great sacrifice for us as a family.
However, after talking with the therapist and my husband, we
decided it was an investment in our future. Looking back now,
it was truly one of the best investments we ever made.

Through therapy, I realized I must go through the step of
confrontation with my parents. Initially, I resisted God's
prompting, but eventually knew that confrontation was part
of God's plan for my healing. The therapist and I spent several
weeks talking about many of the things we have been discussing here. He and I talked about who needed to be confronted,
when it should be done and what it should include.

Having equipped myself through the step of separation,
the beginnings of a new self-image and an accurate image of
God, and through some specialized therapy, I was finally ready
for the confrontation.

What Should Confrontation Include?

In therapy, it became evident that initially I needed to bring
my mother face to face with these issues. During the year of
separation, I saw her five times. She knew I was in therapy.
After phoning, I sent her some material on incest and asked
her to read it. I told her I would be getting together with her

soon to discuss what had been happening in my life and some issues that concerned her.

Prior to seeing her, I sat down and made a list of all the things for which I felt she was accountable. These included ways she set the scene for the incest, as well as issues not directly related to the incest. Mom fostered secrecy by advising us not to ask Dad's permission to do things until it was the "right time." She encouraged me to take showers with my stepfather as a preadolescent. She played the mediator between Dad and us kids and modeled some manipulative behavior that was borderline deception. I discussed all these areas with her openly, sharing how destructive these had been in my life as a child and how I had carried them into my adult life as a wife and mother. For many victims, myself included, our anger with our mother has to do with the whole idea of her inability or unwillingness to protect us.

One victim recalls that when she told her mother about her father's advances, her mother shrugged it off, saying, "Men will be men." Another victim's mother refused to believe her and in essence blamed the victim for acting seductively. There were some mothers who were genuinely unaware of what was happening in the home; however, they were not in touch with the signals given by the child and had in reality put blinders on.

When confronting either the aggressor or a co-contributor it is necessary to have a format. I had two basic outlines I used in talking with my parents individually. The first was very simple. I wanted to start out with the *purpose* of our talk. Second, I presented the *problem*, past and present. Third, I shared the *plan* for resolution. I asked my mother to meet with me one evening and I began by sharing my purpose. I explained that I desired to resolve some issues of the past and for this I requested her support. We discussed briefly the incest material I had sent her and I shared with her that past and present problems had been created by the incest. I enumerated in detail the areas for which I felt she was responsible. Although she was a bit resistive, I continued to state her accountability in the events of the past and the need for her to be responsible. Finally, I explained that total resolution could be accomplished by confronting my stepfather and for that I would appreciate her support and cooperation. I told her I would meet with them together in two days and asked her to tell my stepdad.

How Can It Be Accomplished?

The evening before I was to see them, I phoned to confirm the appointment. My mother answered and I asked if 10 A.M. would be all right. She excused herself from the phone and returned, saying, "Your dad has plans and won't be home!" It was obvious she had not done as I asked. I was outraged! I hung up the phone and realized he was attempting to gain control again. I spoke with my husband, uttered a quick prayer, and immediately called back. My mother answered again and I asked to speak with my stepfather. She said, "I don't think that would be a good idea." I insisted. When he got on the phone I asked him calmly but firmly, "Dad, is what you have to do so important that you could not reschedule it?"

He simply said, "I'm sorry, I have plans."

I repeated my question.

Again he said, "I'm busy."

Finally I said, "Dad, are you refusing to see me?"

By this time, he was agitated. "Well, I have been planning to take your brother to the hardware store for weeks but if you have to come, I guess I can be here!" He followed with a classic statement, "I don't know why we have to discuss this anyway. I thought you were a good enough Christian to have forgiven and forgotten this by now."

Instead of being sidetracked by his attempt to plant blame,

I calmly responded, "Well, Dad, we will talk about all those things tomorrow." I was somewhat relieved. I had asserted my strength and had again gained control. I called a friend and asked her to pray for me the following day. I prayed for knowledge and understanding in responding to my dad's accusatory statement.

I had spent a great deal of time preparing for the confrontation with my stepfather. Since I had failed three times before, I was anxious about it. However, I knew the Lord had prepared the way.

The "how" of the confrontation was as important as the "what." My second outline, specifically designed for my stepfather, was derived from a Bible study on Philemon which I'd heard from Florence Littauer. I knew it would be necessary to begin in a positive manner so that Dad's defenses would not be raised. Therefore, I began with a *compliment*. Because my stepfather was a Christian, attending church had been a weekly activity in our home. We attended a Bible-believing, fundamental church and it was there that I received Christ. I told my dad that I was thankful because had it not been for his influence, I might not know my Jesus. I complimented him for helping me strive for excellence and for two or three other areas in which he had been especially helpful. After the *compliments*, I *confessed* specific incidents in which I had been critical and unkind toward him and asked for his forgiveness. I did not elaborate on either of these points but utilized them to set a positive environment. I then proceeded to answer the statement he had made the night before on the phone. I said, "Dad, you know you said last night that you thought I was a good enough Christian to have forgotten this whole thing. I prayed about that and the Lord gave me an answer. The Lord could have healed that ten-year-old little girl instantaneously had He wanted to. But, you know, He didn't do that. He allowed me to carry this burden for nearly twenty years so that today you could experience His forgiveness at the same time I extend you my forgiveness."

Third, I *confronted* him with his acts. I shared with him briefly that I had confronted Mother in the areas of her responsibilities. Then I talked about the first incestuous incident. He immediately responded with denial, saying, "I don't remember."

I replied firmly. "It does not matter whether you deny it or not. You did molest me. I remember what occurred. It happened to me. I am the victim."

I continued to describe the actual event in detail. I asked him if he remembered molesting my older sister. He turned white and in a low voice he said, "I do remember that."

I said, "Fine. I am not here to confront you on those issues, but on my own." I told him he was *totally* responsible for what had happened and that I was innocent. When he interrupted, I told him I was not finished and that he would have a chance to respond when I was done. I shared all the past and present symptoms I had experienced and gave an example of each. I told him he was responsible for those as well. For example, I had difficulty being open and responsive sexually to my husband. The root, of course, was the incest. My self-esteem was very low and I remembered that he had told me once that no one would be interested in me just for me, but would always have "ulterior" sexual motives. I shared about my nightmares, depression, feelings of guilt, anger and critical spirit. I expressed my feelings about an incident in church the night I accepted Christ at age ten. My sister and I had gone to church by ourselves. During the service I felt the tug of God's Spirit on my heart and raised my hand at the invitation, indicating my desire to know Christ as my Savior. The pastor encouraged those who had made a decision to go to the prayer room. As a result, I kept my stepdad waiting in the car. When I arrived at the car my dad angrily asked, "Where have you been?"

I joyfully exclaimed, "Dad, I asked Jesus into my heart tonight!"

His cold and insensitive response echoed in my head for years. "Why didn't you *wait* until your mother and I were there?" He had taken the most important decision I would ever make and turned it into something negative. As I shared this incident, I was in tears and, for the first time in years, he began to cry. I continued sharing several examples of his overall rejecting attitude toward me in recent years and how devastating this had been to me.

After spending about an hour and a half with the compliment, confess, and confront stages, I began to share my fourth point. I told him my desire was to resolve totally these issues in my life, but in order to do so he must take complete responsibility for what he had done. I told him I was not going to carry that burden any longer. Finally, I expressed my willingness to *commit* myself to rebuilding our relationship. I lovingly told both my parents I wished to have their love and support for me and for their grandchildren. I reminded them, however, that they must take an active part in restoring our relationship if it were to improve, and that it would take some time. My stepdad, for the first time in twenty years, looked me straight in the eyes and said, "Jan, it was all my fault. I take full responsibility for all that happened. Will you forgive me?"

I burst into tears, ran over and hugged my dad, and cried, "Yes, I will." At that time the anxiety, anger, and animosity toward him disappeared. Forgiveness was finally in view. The Lord's presence was there that day; it was the beginning of a positive phase in my life. I could feel a new sense of healing and I knew the best was ahead.

Does Confrontation Always Work?

Some of you probably are saying, "That's nice for Jan, but I bet it doesn't always turn out that way." You are right. Many times the aggressor continues to deny his responsibility. What then? *I believe healing is possible for all victims, whether or not they confront and regardless of the aggressor's response.* Let me deal with the latter situation first. In order to have the issues resolved, it is absolutely necessary for the victim to resolve them within *herself.* That is why the preliminary work of separation, reaching a position of strength, working on the image of self and God is so important. Confrontation validates what the victim already knows to be true. *Her healing, however, is not dependent upon the aggressor's response.* Think of yourself as carrying a load around on your back for years. You finally realize you have carried this load for the aggressor and you decide it is time to unload it. In the confrontation, you take the load off your own back and place it at his feet. You don't have to wait to see if he picks it up. Remember, it is not your responsibility to carry it any longer.

I know of one woman who confronted her father and was met with denial. Despite his reaction, she walked away free because she had resolved it within herself. Although her father was still in denial and disinterested in reconciliation, she could experience healing because she had done her part.

When the perpetrator denies the truth, the victim must decide whether or not to continue the relationship. I recommend that she clearly state that his denial makes it obvious that he is not interested in reconciliation. She may then say to him, "Until you are willing to face your accountability for what you have done, there can be no relationship." Under these circumstances, the choice remains with the aggressor. The issue is resolved for the victim, but, due to the aggressor's choice, the relationship cannot be reconciled.

Confrontation is an individual matter and the results will vary. Healing is possible even if a face-to-face confrontation does not take place. Certainly, our Lord would not restrict healing to only those who confront directly; otherwise, the

victim whose aggressor is deceased would be without hope.
Through alternative confrontation methods, such as role-playing and other therapeutic techniques, healing can be achieved.

Most victims who have contact with their offenders find
confrontation necessary. I recommend a face-to-face meeting
rather than a letter in most cases, if safety or distance is not an
issue. Many victims have effectively used a letter in conjunc-
tion with a face-to-face confrontation as a validation of what
was discussed.

One timid young woman in my support group had a great
deal of trouble over this issue of confrontation. She finally
decided to phone her father, the aggressor, and tell him she
had had it. "I'm paying for individual therapy sessions and
attending a support group forty miles away. As a result my
husband and I are under a great deal of financial pressure." In
a firm, louder-than-normal voice, she used language she knew
her father would understand, then concluded, "And on top of
that, I'm practically frigid because of you!" For the first time,
her father admitted his involvement with her. He volunteered
to pay for her therapy and seemed to realize he was responsible
for that compensation because he had injured her.

Remember, confrontation is bringing people face to face
with the issues, and should be done with the motive of reconciliation. Confrontation may be necessary to place the responsibility in the hands of the rightful owners. It is scriptural, and
can benefit the aggressor as well as the victim. Finally, it is a
means of breaking the incestuous pattern. We have seen that
confrontation involves not only the aggressor but also may
include any other person who has been a co-contributor.

We have discussed in detail the importance of when the
confrontation should occur and the preliminary steps that are
so important. Developing your position of strength is imperative. Separation from the aggressor also may be a needed
ingredient. Laying a new foundation for your self-image and

an accurate image of God are vital for success. Finally, seeking specialized therapy or participating in a support group can provide the additional assistance you need.

We detailed that the format of the confrontation should include: a purpose, a description of the problem, and the presentation of a plan. The how of the confrontation was achieved by keeping in mind the need to compliment and confess in an attempt to set a positive environment for the confrontation.

The confrontation itself was specific, detailing the incestuous incident as well as any other symptomatic by-products for which the aggressor was responsible. Finally, there was the expressed desire for a new commitment which resulted in healing for the victim and the aggressor.

Many of the victims I work with ask me. "Will I ever be totally healed? Will the emotional pain ever lessen? Will I ever be able to forgive him for what he did to me?" To all these questions I answer an unequivocal, "Yes! Having confronted the aggressor directly or within the therapeutic environment, you are one major step further. The pathway to forgiveness is just ahead. If you are feeling that you are not quite there yet, take heart. You are not alone."

PRACTICAL INSIGHTS

1. Write down what you wish to say in the confrontation. Remember to be specific about the incident and detail the by-products you've experienced as a result, i.e., sexual problems in marriage, low self-esteem, depression, etc. Read the paper to your therapist or a knowledgeable support person and get feedback. Make any adjustments necessary. If you will be confronting directly, pray that the Holy Spirit will give you discernment as to the appropriate timing. Rehearse the

confrontation several times in front of the mirror or in the presence of someone else. Watch what your body language is communicating nonverbally. It is important that your body language be congruent with your verbal message.

2. Read 2 Samuel 12. Allow the Holy Spirit to speak to you about the benefits to be gained through confrontation. Remember even after the sin, David is still known as "a man after God's own heart."

3. Memorize Psalm 29:11 and Psalm 31:24.

CHAPTER 9

Step VIII:
Acknowledge Forgiveness

Forgive and forget. A lofty goal! Or is it? One Christian speaker said, "The challenge is not to forgive and forget. The real honor comes in one's ability to forgive and yet remember."

The women I counsel come to me in various stages of despair. Several have been advised by pastors, deacons and well-meaning Christians to simply forgive. They have been assured by their counselors that an instantaneous healing of their emotions will occur. Unfortunately, this is not always the case. When there is no evidence of such a miraculous healing, these counselors are quick to point out that the injured person is no doubt responsible. For the victim this becomes a devastating cycle.

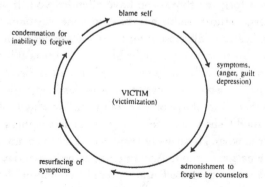

blame self

condemnation for
inability to forgive

symptoms,
(anger, guilt
depression)

VICTIM
(victimization)

resurfacing of
symptoms

admonishment to
forgive by counselors

Forgiveness, like many other areas in our Christian life, is a process. It may be that you can truly and totally forgive your husband for making an unkind statement a minute after he makes it. For some it takes longer. The deeper the wound inflicted, the longer the process of forgiveness. This doesn't mean that you are given license to hold on to bitterness, anger and resentment. It does mean that the more serious the injury inflicted, the longer it may take to work through the emotions toward the final goal of forgiveness.

Donna came to our support group one evening, anxious for an opportunity to share a fresh discovery. She told the following story:

I became depressed last week after a counseling session with my pastor. I'd finally gotten the courage to share with him all the events surrounding my background. I'd been molested from age seven to age fifteen by various men my mother brought home. I'd been raped repeatedly by my uncle and several cousins and eventually forced to have an abortion at age fifteen. I shared with my pastor how devastating these events had been on my marriage and about the depression that, at times, seemed insurmountable. When I told him about the anger I had toward my children and husband, the nightmares, and my inability to trust my husband, he stopped me short. He abruptly stated, "Donna, the problem is obvious. You have not forgiven those who have offended you. If you will right now forgive those people who have in some way damaged you, you will be healed of all those symptoms you are describing." I wanted to forgive—in fact, I'd thought I had—but I was still experiencing those same difficulties. I went away in a state of defeat. I thought I was just not spiritual enough. I was destined to live my life in bondage. As I went to work the following Monday I asked the Lord if He might show me something about forgiveness. Boy, was I surprised when He answered that very day! I'm a nurse and I work in the emergency room. A young man came in that day. He had just been run over by a truck and suffered a compound fracture of the leg. The bone was protruding, broken in several places. It took three doctors and two nurses four hours to get the man's bone set in a position to heal. The healing process would take anywhere from four months to a year. Even then, the young man might experience some difficulty in walking and it could take several months more to attain the full use of his injured leg. As I looked at this boy with his leg in a cast, I realized the Lord was using this to illustrate something profound to me. No one at anytime approached that young man and said, "Son, I have good news for you. All you need to do is forgive the man who was driving the truck and you will be instantaneously healed." No one would be so foolish, and yet, how many of us approach emotional brokenness in that same simplistic manner?

As Donna shared that personal answer to prayer, we observed a new sense of freedom in the group members. Many had been so burdened with guilt over their inability to forgive, that it hindered their overall healing process. Our support group served the same function with each victim as the doctors and nurses did with the young patient. We could not accomplish the healing, but we could start victims on their healing process. The doctors set the man's leg but they couldn't heal it. We chart a supportive course, but each woman will heal at her own rate. The Holy Spirit is the only one who accomplishes healing in our lives. We must make certain that we're in a position to receive it!

Family Business

A new part of my personal healing was about to start. Because of the visibility of my ministry to incest victims and an upcoming appearance on *The 700 Club*, members of my family needed to know what I was doing. My parents had indicated previously that they did not want Jim, my twenty-one-year-old half-brother, to know about the molestation. Because Jim had never been exposed to the truth, he had a number of misconceptions about why my older sister Kathy had left home abruptly when he was five years old and why my stepdad and I had always had such a difficult relationship. Since my brother had completed his college education and had recently recommitted his life to Christ, I began praying about whether or not to inform him of the molestation. After several months of prayer and counseling with others, I felt this was a necessary step; however, I could not let my parents know I was going to tell him or they would approach him first and minimize the seriousness of these situations.

As I set up a time to talk with my brother, my anxiety level was especially high. What would it do to him? How would he feel about me? About Dad and Mom? What kind of reaction would he have? Although these questions concerned me, I felt an inner peace. I knew God was leading me. As I met with Jim in my kitchen one spring day, I began with prayer and then shared what God had been doing in my life. I told Jim how God had used me to form and lead support groups for women, how God had done a tremendous emotional healing in my life and how I would be appearing on *The 700 Club* to talk about that healing.

Then delicately and softly, I said, "Jim, you may wonder why this information concerns you. When I was ten years old, Dad molested me." Instantly tears welled up in his eyes and anger flashed across his face. Before he had a chance to speak I continued, "Jim, I don't want to hurt you, but you have a right to know these things. First, my ministry is expanding in such a way that you might hear this second hand and I didn't want that to happen. Second, because you might marry some day and have children, you need to be aware that Dad has never sought help about his problem and that he has the potential of molesting again. I could not live with myself if you were not told about this possibility. Also, that is why I will not leave my girls alone with him and Mom. Third, because of the environment in which you grew up you, too, have the potential of molesting your own children."

His immediate response was understandable. "Your going on TV could ruin Dad and Mom's lives."

Instead of being defensive, I merely said, "I understand what you must be feeling." In the next few minutes I shared the motivation behind my actions. I explained my intent was not to defame our parents in any way, but to offer hope and healing to thousands of others who also had been victimized. I shared 2 Corinthians 1:4 which says God "comforts us in all our tribulation, that we may be able to comfort those who are in any trouble, with the comfort with which we ourselves are comforted by God." I told Jim the specifics of how God had led me into this ministry and how this might be an opportunity to restore our family. We discussed the proper timing to tell our parents that Jim was aware of the past. We decided it was best that I approach them first with a follow-up visit by Jim. I encouraged him to reaffirm his love to our parents, reminding Jim that my goal was to unite our family, not divide it. Jim responded by saying, "If you can forgive Dad for what he's done to you, I certainly can too." From that day until this Jim and I have shared a deeper bond than we had ever known.

Next, I went to see my parents. As we sat in their living room, I shared how the Lord had led me into the support groups and into speaking. I told them about the upcoming *700 Club* appearance and how the Lord was using the hurts and healing in my life to offer hope to others. I expressed my concern for them due to the visibility of my ministry, but confidently stated that I wished to be obedient to what the Lord was placing on my heart. I assured them that my emphasis was not on what had happened but on what God had done through the healing process. I told them I had done a cassette tape for Word Publishers which included my testimony and steps to healing. I openly shared that although I was specific in naming my stepfather as the offender and sharing some specifics of my mother's role, I was always sensitive never to mention a location or names.

I paused and gave my parents a chance to respond. My stepdad's comment was, "You have to do what you have to do." My mother reluctantly echoed his reply.

I told them that I had already informed my brother of the situation. Dad and Mother immediately burst into tears. In the past, this reaction would have made me feel guilty, but because of my new strength I was able to continue. I shared compassionately with my dad that every time I'd prayed for him over the past few years the Lord had shown me a picture of a little boy in a dark closet, crying. I said, "Dad, I'm not sure what that means, but I think you know."

The tears flowed down his face. It was clear that God had been the originator of that mental picture. My dad then related to me something he had bottled up for years. "Just yesterday I told your mother what happened to me when I was fourteen. I was molested by our church youth director. I have never forgotten that."

Then I spoke directly to my dad about forgiveness. Dad had told me at the original confrontation that he had been pleading for years that the Lord would forgive him. I took this opportunity to tell Dad that the reason he had not experienced forgiveness was he had failed to follow the biblical prescription in Matthew 5:23-24: "Therefore if you bring your gift to the altar, and there remember that your brother has something against you, leave your gift there before the altar, and go your way. First be reconciled to your brother, and then come and offer your gift."

When I had confronted him and he had asked for my forgiveness, we were reconciled. However, he had never gone to my older sister, Kathy, to ask her forgiveness. I paraphrased the following story from Chuck Swindoll's book *Improving Your Serve*,[1] for my stepdad:

> Let's say I am driving away from your church parking lot next Sunday morning. I back my car into the side of your beautiful Mercedes 450 SEL. CRUNCH! You are visiting with friends following the service and you hear the noise. Your stomach churns as you see me get out of the car, look at the damage and then bow in prayer and say, "Dear Lord, please forgive me for being so preoccupied and clumsy. And please give John grace as he sees the extensive damage I have caused out of sheer negligence. And provide his needs as he takes this car in to have it fixed. Thanks, Lord. Amen." As I drive away, I wave and smile real big as I yell out the window, "It's all cleared up, John. I claimed the damage before God. Isn't grace wonderful?"

I told Dad how necessary it was for him to go to the one he has offended. I urged him not to do it for me, but to pray and depend on God's leading and timing. I spent the balance of the time encouraging both parents to seek counseling themselves, and I left Josh McDowell's self-image book *His Image . . . My Image*, for them to read. I expressed my love to both of them and, our eyes filled with tears, we hugged. I told them I knew God desired to restore our family and that openness was a key to that restoration.

Two months later my sister Kathy phoned to tell me she had received the call from our stepfather that she had been wanting for nearly twenty-five years. Over the phone he had sobbed, "Please forgive me for all that I've done to you. I've been praying for several weeks and know that I can be forgiven by God if you will just forgive me." Kathy could hardly believe it! She had always hoped that call would come some day, but she had resigned herself to the fact that it probably never would.

She answered, "What you did has seriously affected my life. If it hadn't been for Jan's help, I wouldn't have made it.

We've begun to deal with the problem together. Dad, I hope this will be the new start for our family that I've wanted. I'm willing to forgive you."

I waited a day and called my dad to reaffirm my love. God was working in our family and now Dad could have the assurance of God's forgiveness since he had followed the biblical prescription for reconciliation. I suggested that we sit down now as a family and have a family meeting, not to rehash what had happened to us as children, but once and for all to share openly about the incest with all immediate family members and spouses. I told him the goal was merely to lay it on the table since everyone knew anyway and use it as a time to talk about a plan for a restoration. Dad was hesitant, reluctant. My mother was extremely resistive and said, "There's no point." I became frustrated and tried to share how this could be a new beginning for us as a family. She was defensive. I accused her of still being in denial and never really coming to grips with her own responsibility in the whole series of events. When I hung up that day I was convinced I was right and was a bit angry over their lack of enthusiasm for a family meeting.

My brother, Jim, called the next day, and he added further insight. He and my parents had had a blow-up which was the catalyst that prompted my dad's call to Kathy.

Jim said, "Mom and Dad don't like the family meeting idea, and according to them, Kathy doesn't either."

I asked, "Jim, what do you think?"

He replied, "I told them I thought it was a good idea."

I hung up feeling depressed and betrayed. I thought the Holy Spirit had been working in my dad's heart, leading him to make that call to Kathy. Now I knew that my brother had forced my dad's hand. I felt betrayed by my sister who originally had agreed to a family meeting. Obviously, Kathy had changed her mind. When she phoned a few days later, I asked her about the family meeting. She said, "Well, at first I thought it was a good idea, but now I just don't think we should push it any further."

Later that week, I received the same response from my mother. I informed her that I wouldn't force the issue, but that I believed healing could only be accomplished by bringing things into the open. The week that followed was one of the most intense weeks I have ever experienced. God's hand was heavy upon me. I had been reading a book on inner healing and resisting some of the concepts it presented regarding forgiveness. But I opened up enough to say, "If I'm being stubborn or defiant in this area, Lord, please show me. I want to be obedient to what You desire." The Lord never fails to hear such prayers and He began to speak to me. He laid on my heart how rigid I was and how I was not showing forgiveness to my parents, yet expecting so much from them.

My flesh was arguing with God like Jacob struggled with the angel. "But I am right, Lord. They need to do this! If I show any weakness, or compromise my position, they will think I have changed my mind." I argued for several days. On the seventh day I woke up feeling compelled to go to the Scripture. I was immediately drawn to Matthew 23:4 where Jesus speaks about the Pharisees: "They tie up heavy loads, hard to bear, and place them on mens' shoulders, but they themselves will not lift a finger to help bear them" (Amplified Bible). I went on to read the "woes" Jesus pronounced on the Pharisees and felt God's Spirit saying, "Jan, you are just like them."

Still resisting, I phoned a friend who has children my age; I knew she could give me wisdom from her mother's heart. As I shared the circumstances, Alyson sweetly but confidently said, "Jan, I think you need to love your parents. What they need right now more than anything is their daughter's love. You must love them in spite of the fact that from our human standpoint they don't deserve it."

I burst into tears. I knew she was right. My flesh argued,

saying, "But we do need a family meeting and if I back down they are going to think everything is okay."

Alyson tenderly asked, "Jan, can you love them if they never have that meeting?"

I told her, "I don't know."

After hanging up the phone, I opened the Word and began randomly reading in 2 Chronicles 30. The Spirit had my assignment all prepared. The question was, would I listen? As I read this portion of Scripture, it became clear to me why the Holy Spirit had led me to it. Hezekiah had ordered the restoration of the temple worship. He was attempting to reestablish God's law in Israel and Judah. Along with the reinstituting of the law, Hezekiah made a decree that the people should come to Jerusalem to celebrate the Passover. In chapter 30, they are making preparation for the celebration. Verses 7-9 jumped off the page at me as I read.

> And do not be like your fathers and your brethren, who trespassed against the LORD God of their fathers, so that He gave them up to desolation, as you see. Now do not be *stiff-necked*, as your fathers were, but yield yourselves to the LORD; and enter His sanctuary, which He has sanctified forever, and serve the LORD your God, that the fierceness of His wrath may turn away from you. For if you return to the LORD, your brethren and your children will be treated with compassion by those who lead them captive, so that they may come back to this land; for the LORD your God is gracious and merciful, and will not turn His face from you if you return to Him (emphasis mine).

It was apparent that the Lord was calling me to yield, not to be stiff-necked, and the result would be His compassion on my family. Verses 18-20 continued,

> For a multitude of the people, many from Ephraim, Manasseh, Issachar, and Zebulun, had not cleansed themselves, yet they ate the Passover contrary to what was written. *But Hezekiah prayed for them, saying,* "May the good LORD provide atonement for everyone

who prepares his heart to seek God, the LORD God of his fathers, though he is not cleansed according to the purification of the sanctuary." And the LORD listened to Hezekiah, and healed the people (emphasis mine).

Hezekiah knew the people had not done what they should have regarding purification. But instead of holding them to the letter of the law, he interceded in their behalf.

As I sat humbled before the Lord that day, He showed me my two alternatives. I could remain a Pharisee, adhering to the letter of the law, which would be a justifiable position, or I could be a Hezekiah bridging the gap through intercession for my family.

Who are you today? Are you a person who holds on to your rights and demands that others respect you and follow through? Or are you a Hezekiah who knows what should be done, but chooses out of love to intercede for others that they might receive healing? As God's Spirit touched me that day, I lay face down on the floor in our study crying out to God, "But Lord, they owe me!"

The Lord's strong, tender voice resounded in my heart, "Yes, Jan, they do. But are you willing to release them of their debt?"

I honestly responded, "Lord, I don't know if I can, but I'm willing if You'll work out that release in my heart."

I concluded that day with the reading in Matthew 18:21-35. It is the parable of the king who had a servant who owed him several million dollars. The servant begged for mercy from the king and the Scripture says in verse 27 that the king was "moved with compassion, released him, and forgave him the debt." That same servant went out and found someone who owed him a mere 15 dollars and demanded immediate payment. The debtor asked for mercy, but it was denied and he was cast into prison. Others who observed both events went to the king and told him how the servant had failed to have compassion. In verse 34 we read: "And his master was angry, and delivered him to the torturers."

Although I had read this parable many times, it took on new meaning that day. I had to make the choice. I could be the "gracious lord" or the "unforgiving servant." There was no question who I wanted to be. The release came when I knelt down to intercede for my parents. When I prayed for God's blessing upon them, I felt a new sense of freedom for myself. As long as I hung on to that bitterness and unforgiving attitude, I was subject to being "delivered to the torturers." Now I no longer wished to be held captive. I released my parents from their debt and released myself into the arms of a Lord who is full of grace and mercy. That day I began a new commitment to walk in the freedom of forgiveness. I had a fresh desire to express my love to my parents in a tangible way by sending them a gift certificate for dinner at one of their favorite restaurants. I am still convinced a family meeting would be a healthy step toward wholeness in our family, but I am just as convinced that I am to love them regardless of their response.

This experience showed me that forgiveness is a fourfold process. First, I must acknowledge or own up to the pain. Second, I must release my right to hold on to bitterness, resentment and anger. Third, I must desire reconciliation. Fourth, I must extend to the offender an invitation to rebuild the relationship through the expression of unconditional love and acceptance. Before we look at the four stages in detail, we should understand that forgiveness is a process. Many times Christians are admonished to jump quickly to stage four, but they soon discover that the acceptance is a superficial covering that hides underlying feelings which still cause pain.

The Lord used an event of several years ago to illustrate this concept in my life. When I was eighteen I had four impacted wisdom teeth removed. The painful procedure required a general anesthetic. The oral surgeon had to dig out the impacted teeth, resulting in several days of pain, swelling and eating difficulties. Several weeks after the swelling went down, I again experienced pain and discomfort. I returned to the surgeon for a recheck. He examined my mouth and said, "You have developed a dry socket." He explained that a dry socket is caused when the blood clot is dislodged and bone is exposed. In my case, a layer of skin had formed, prematurely covering the wound. I had healed superficially on the outside, but underneath dried blood and food particles had caused an infection, which was the reason for my pain. The oral surgeon lanced the wound again and cleaned it out. He showed me how to inject the wound with saline solution using a hypodermic needle. He warned me this would be a slow, painful process, and that I must now heal from the inside out. It took several weeks and many unpleasant sessions with the needle for the discomfort to disappear and the infection to heal.

This process is much like the experience we often have as Christian victims. The wound has become deeply embedded and impacted. Even if we have attempted to dig it out over time, we tend to leave some residue, and covering it over with a superficial layer of apparent forgiveness. We didn't take the time to heal properly by extracting all the emotions and hurts associated with the wound. As a result, we develop a dry socket in our life. We exhibit symptoms of an unresolved wound. We must begin the lengthy, painful process of laying the wound open and ridding ourselves of the infectious material—the second step in the process of forgiveness. We fail to recognize the signs and we live under the pretense that recovery has taken place.

At one recent seminar, Karen Burton Maines spoke on the topic, "Lies." She said, "The fictions we create for ourselves often inhibit our growth."

Have you created a fiction? Have you applied a superficial forgiveness to a past hurt? Has a dry socket developed in your life? Will you uncover it and work at getting rid of the internal infection? Until you do, complete healing cannot take place.

So many of us are unwilling to forgive. It is partly because we really don't understand that it is a process. Our reluctance also stems from a misinterpretation of what forgiveness is. Many feel that it says to the offender, "What you did was okay." Because of this misinterpretation, many people find it impossible to extend forgiveness.

Let's look closely now at each step of the process. As we saw in Matthew 18, forgiveness conveys the idea of "sending away" or "letting go," a releasing. What is it that the offended person releases? She releases her right to hold on to anger, bitterness and resentment. She releases the offender of the debt. This in no way means that the victim has condoned or even justified the offender's actions. Rather, the victim releases her right to hold on to some justified emotions which were evoked by the offender and his actions.

In order for that releasing to take place, the offended person must first recognize the possession of such emotions. That is why it is so necessary for the victim to relive the feelings associated with being victimized.

In *Healing of Memories*, David Seamands writes, "The harder we try to keep bad memories out of conscious recall, the more powerful they become. Since they are not allowed to enter through the door of our minds directly, they come into our personalities (body, mind and spirit) in disguised and destructive ways."[2] The first step toward breaking the bondage of our past is acknowledging or owning up to the pain.

Acknowledging/Owning the Pain

Somehow, we have failed in the Christian community to incorporate the acknowledgment of our pain as an essential part of forgiveness.

Suppose you find out from a friend that Gertrude Gossip,

a woman in your Bible study, has been flagrantly revealing personal information you shared with her in confidence, distorting the information and placing you in an unfavorable light. You find out that she has done this all during your friendship with her the past three months. You are angry and hurt. You can't believe she would repeat these intimate conversations, much less lie about the details. Yet when you see Gertrude you avoid her, smiling sweetly on the outside while you're seething on the inside. One Tuesday morning Gertrude approaches you. She tells you what she has done and genuinely asks for your forgiveness. You reply rather quickly, "Oh, it's all right— it's no big deal. Let's be friends." In your mind you are telling yourself you have done what "good Christians do"—forgiving seventy times seven.

Several destructive elements are at work in this situation. First, there has been a total denial of the intense hurt and anger you experienced. By not acknowledging this hurt openly with Gertrude, you leave yourself wide open for the root of bitterness to spring up in your heart. By not telling her how her actions made you feel, you will have a tendency to distrust her every time you see her whispering to another woman. You will probably unconsciously maintain a distance between you for safety's sake. As Chuck Swindoll put it in a recent sermon, "You will keep Gertrude on 'probationary' status. She will never be fully forgiven, but you will 'subject her to a period of testing and trial to ascertain her fitness.'"

The second destructive element is that of minimizing her actions. This may inadvertently reinforce what she had done. You invalidate her repentance. Think of how difficult it must have been for Gertrude to muster up the courage to confess her faults before you and ask you for your forgiveness. What do you think it does to her when you say, "Oh, it's okay. It was no big deal. It didn't matter much to me anyway"? You may unknowingly nullify the work of the Holy Spirit in her life.

What would be a proper response to Gertrude's apology? You might approach it this way. "Thank you, Gertrude, for coming to me. I was hurt and angry when I heard the things you were telling others about me. You betrayed my trust. I'd like to forgive you, but it will probably take some time. However, I'm willing to work toward forgiveness and restoration." Do you see the difference? This interchange was real instead of superficial. How we need this as Christians.

Consider why Christ's death on the cross has so much value. The value of His death and the forgiveness He extends to us has a great deal to do with the pain that He suffered. It cost Him something. Had the cross been easy, forgiveness would not have the value that it does. The Scripture emphasizes the grief and pain He endured on our behalf and the forgiveness available to us as a result.

In acknowledging our pain we validate forgiveness. Seamands writes, "In many instances, there can be no true healing and spiritual growth until we are released from the painful memories and unhealthy patterns which now interfere with our present attitudes and behavior."[3] In denying our pain we give opportunity to the enemy. We may try to deny our feelings, but we will live them out daily, and they will assume other names.

If true healing is to occur, we must be willing to face and acknowledge the pain we suffered at the hand of the offender. It is in knowing that pain and working through it that forgiveness becomes a priceless gift offered to the one who has hurt us.

Releasing Your Rights
As you read these words, you may feel an inner struggle. Have you been hurt deeply by someone you love? Have you subconsciously said to yourself, "I will never trust him again"? If so, you need to come to grips with this step of releasing. As

I shared earlier, I was stubbornly resistive to this step. I had determined I was justified in keeping up my guard and in maintaining my rights as the injured person. The Lord used Matthew 18:18 to show me what I was doing. In this verse, Jesus said, "Whatever you bind on earth will be bound in heaven, and whatever you loose on earth will be loosed in heaven." By my unwillingness to release my rights, I was binding up both my parents and myself. As long as the offender remained bound to me, I was actually inhibiting God's ability to work in his life, or in my own.

You have met people who exuded bitterness from every pore, miserable souls who spend a lifetime rehashing old hurts, retelling conversations and reliving their pain with no intention of releasing it. Often they are people who, when asked or confronted about their anger, deny its existence. Nevertheless, it is evident to all.

In *Growing Strong in the Seasons of Life*, Chuck Swindoll puts it this way:

> You cannot nurture the bitterness root and at the same time keep it concealed. The bitter root bears bitter fruit. You may think you can hide it . . . live with it, grin and bear it, but you cannot. Slowly, inexorably, that sharp, cutting edge of unforgiveness will work its way to the surface.[4]

Releasing may take time. It may or may not be a once and for all act. I think Joseph in the Old Testament represents a person in this process. Many pastors and speakers draw upon Joseph as the exemplary victim in the Old Testament. They tell you how he was sold into slavery by his jealous brothers and eventually imprisoned. Then they bring you to Joseph's famous words in Genesis 50:20: "You, my brothers, meant this for evil but God meant it for good" (my paraphrase). As you hear those words you wonder if you could have responded in such a virtuous way. I believe this divine response was not borne without some struggle. Although we have no record of Joseph's emotional state during those years of imprisonment, I rather imagine he must have gone through periods of anger, resentment and bitterness. I believe God used those fourteen years in prison to shape Joseph. During that time God molded him and brought him to the resolution of forgiveness. It was not an automatic process.

Many victims are internally imprisoned. The process of forgiveness requires that they acknowledge and own their pain and that they reach a point of being able to release it. It is important that they take time to accomplish that release just as Joseph did. The effects will be far more lasting and will produce a greater result for all concerned.

Desiring Reconciliation

In his book *Reconciliation*, John Edwards Jones writes, "As a lawyer my job is to see that people are treated fairly. But I am not to release them from the consequences of their acts . . . and the same is true as ministers of reconciliation. We are to help people, not remove them from accountability."[5] This concept is so important in understanding the function of forgiveness. Reconciliation does not condone, applaud or rubber-stamp what the offender has done. It seeks harmony or peace between those who have offended and those who have been offended. Yet reconciliation does not deny what has happened or the pain that has resulted.

You will recall from the previous chapter that Ellen, through confrontation, found out that her daughter also had been molested by her father. Because this confrontation took place in the presence of a licensed therapist, the therapist was required by law to inform the authorities of the abuse of the granddaughter. As you can imagine, this was an extremely difficult situation for Ellen. She desired to be reconciled to her father and to forgive him, and yet she had an obligation to her daughter, Karie, and to other children, as her father had the potential of victimizing again. Ellen and I spent a great deal of time discussing her alternatives. She did not want her father imprisoned but she did want him to get help. Because the authorities were involved, she was limited in her choices. Her struggle centered around this question of forgiveness.

She phoned me one day and said, "My mother just called me and accused me of being a phony Christian. She said if I were a true Christian, I would drop everything and just forgive my dad. Jan, is she right? Should I just forgive him and not press this further?" I talked with Ellen in detail about her responsibility. I took her to several Scriptures including 2 Samuel 12 where David is confronted with his sin. In verse 13 he acknowledges his sin and the prophet Nathan tells David the Lord forgives him. In verses 10-12 Nathan pronounced God's judgment upon David's house, saying in effect, "Thus saith the Lord, 'The sword shall never depart from your house. Your wives shall be taken from you and given to your neighbors, the child Bathsheba is carrying will die'" (my paraphrase). God knew David would repent. God also knew He would forgive David. But God did not make removing the natural consequences of David's sin a part of that forgiveness.

As victims, we need to keep this in mind. We are not under obligation to circumvent natural consequences for sin. In fact, it can be detrimental to the offender if we do. God uses consequences in our lives to teach us. As I shared these things with Ellen, she decided to go to her father. She went to him and told him her real desire was that he seek counseling for his problem, not that he go to jail. Her father said he was not willing to seek counseling because he "did not have a problem." She felt that, because of his unwillingness, she needed to let the legal system take its course. As a result her father was arrested, convicted and placed on probation. As a part of his probation he was required to seek counseling. It has been a difficult season for her family, but Ellen says, "Because I committed this to the Lord, I know He is using this to work in my dad's life." Her daughter, Karie, has been given two clear messages: One, she was not at fault for what happened. Two, her parents loved her and were acting in her behalf to protect her from any further victimization. These two messages are vital in restoring the damage that Karie has experienced.

The Scripture is so clear on this issue. We have been reconciled to God through Christ. God never denies the sin that has held us captive. He acknowledges the pain endured by His Son, releases those of us who have personally accepted His provision, and reconciles us to Himself. Many times we, like David, will reap the consequences of what we have sown, even as Christians. As you seek reconciliation with the offender, remember, "Reconciliation does not mean we eliminate the consequences of sin from people's lives. It means we help them through the consequences so that they may be totally healed."[6]

Rebuilding the Relationship

For many, the process of rebuilding is a difficult one. Too often, old patterns of relating and communicating hinder the ability to start anew. Sometimes the offender is not interested in rebuilding the relationship. The offended person must remember that she is accountable only for herself. To build a relationship, it takes two active participants. As the injured person, she is responsible only for her half.

As I shared earlier, the first step God required of me — after I had acknowledged my pain, released the bitterness and resentment, and sought reconciliation — was demonstrating love to my parents tangibly. As Christians, we often think we must feel the emotion before we can act. We fear the accusation of being hypocritical, so we fail to respond in the absence of the proper emotion. Scripturally, we are commanded to act in spite of the emotion we may feel. In fact, psychologists tell us that the determination to act and the act itself often precipitate the appropriate emotion.

There is a distinct difference between hypocrisy and following a scriptural prescription in the absence of emotion. It all has to do with motive. The Pharisees, who were confronted with their hypocrisy constantly by Jesus, set out to pretend they were something they were not. The follower of Christ realizes from the beginning that he does not feel the proper emotion before he chooses to act, but he desires a harmony between his will and his emotions. He does not pretend with God or others. For many who have been victimized the area of their will has suffered devastating effects. They often find they are unable to make new choices because at a very early age they were stripped of their right to choose for themselves.

Joanne was a case in point. She had been victimized by several people throughout her life. Through group therapy, she began to acknowledge her pain and was trying to release some of the anger she felt toward her mother for allowing her to be victimized. Her relationship with her mother had always been stormy. Because her mother often accused her of being "unstable and crazy," Joanne had difficulty sifting through what her responsibilities were, both to herself and to her mother. We have found in working with Joanne and others that self-image is the key to restoring relationships. We will look at this in greater detail in the next chapter as we see how injured people must begin to rebuild their self-image before they can effectively rebuild relationships with others.

PRACTICAL INSIGHTS

1. Acknowledge your pain by checking any of the following feelings you experienced as a result of being victimized:

ashamed	☐	confused	☐	angry	☐
insecure	☐	hateful	☐	sad	☐
dissappointed	☐	resentful	☐	lonely	☐
fearful	☐	numb	☐	disgusted	☐
powerless	☐	trapped	☐	in pain	☐
embarrassed	☐	frightened	☐	dirty	☐

others_____

Over the next few weeks or months consider the following steps:

A. Taking ownership: Identify these feelings as your own, and assess how they have impacted your life through the suffering they caused.

B. Releasing your rights: As you look over your list, knowing the intensity of what you felt, can you now ask the Lord to help you release any anger, bitterness or resentment that lingers in the depths of your heart?

C. Reconciling: Picture the blood of Jesus that was shed on your behalf and apply that blood to the sin of the offender.

D. Rebuilding relationships: Choose one act of kindness that you can extend to your offender in sincerity. Choose something that will genuinely demonstrate your love to him.

2. Read Matthew 18:21-35. Confess any remaining unforgiveness and ask the Holy Spirit to flood you with His love and His acceptance of the offender. Ask to be able to see the offender through the eyes of Jesus.

3. Memorize Colossians 3:13.

CHAPTER 10

Step IX:

Rebuild Self-image and Relationships

In his book *His Image... My Image*, Josh McDowell defines a healthy self-image as "seeing yourself as God sees you — no more and no less."[1] Do you really view yourself as God views you? Many influences contribute to the picture we have of ourselves: our background, our relationship with our parents or mates, our religious experiences, and a multitude of other factors.

Josh McDowell sees our self-image as a three-legged stool. He contends that "three basic emotional needs are common to all persons." These are:

1. The need to feel loved, accepted; to have a sense of belonging.

2. The need to feel acceptable; to have a sense of worthiness.

3. The need to feel adequate; to have a sense of competence.[2]

If we base our self-image solely on any one of these areas, we have a "stool" that cannot stand. In my own life, I never felt a sense of worth or belonging, so I compensated in the area of competence. I became an overachiever who could point to my accomplishments and say, "You see, I *am* a worthwhile person." The problem with basing our self-image on any one of the three areas is that we use that one area to justify the others. Unfortunately, this does not work. We tend to set up one, or even two, areas as a defensive strategy against the other one. We maintain our defense strategy to cover up what we feel is the real truth about ourselves. For me, under that veneer of competence was a deep sense of unworthiness and the general feeling that "I'm not okay." But this is deceptive. In the realm of the Spirit, I am whole. I am worthy. I am "accepted in the beloved." We must work out in the flesh what has been accomplished already in the Spirit. I am still in this process — but I praise God for His revelation of the truth that I am complete in Him.

As we look at this process of rebuilding our self-image and our relationships, we must keep in mind that we cannot disperse in a day what has taken a lifetime to accumulate. There are three steps in the rebuilding process. First, the victim must *reject* the false notions she has about herself and God. Second, she must begin to *renew* her mind. Third, she must set about to *restore* relationships.

Rejecting Faulty Beliefs

How do you begin rejecting false notions? William Backus and Marie Chapian have written an excellent book entitled *Telling Yourself the Truth*. They discuss the misbelief system that colors our entire world, and they explain, "There are three steps to becoming the happy person you were meant to be:

1. Locate your misbeliefs.

2. Remove them.

3. Replace misbeliefs with truth."[3]

Their first two steps deal with rejecting false notions.

Although I had been a Christian for fifteen years, I had never incorporated the Scriptures that spoke of my value to

God. I knew God loved me as an intellectual truth, but I never internalized it in the depths of my heart. I just believed He was not as pleased with me as He was with others. At that time, when studying the Scriptures I would focus on the negative verses, those that spoke of God's displeasure and judgment. This left me feeling worse than if I had never opened my Bible.

Some of you have done the same thing. Every radio preacher, every sermon or Scripture that begins "Woe unto you" becomes a message intended specifically for you. On the other hand, you think every message that tells of God's acceptance, favor and love is meant for the person in the next pew, certainly not for you!

I was not aware I had trouble in this area until I attended the Bible study on self-worth at my church. I went to that study not knowing that God was starting me on His pathway to healing.

As I began studying there and memorizing His Word, I came to a significant conclusion: Either His Word was totally true or it was not.

I realized I must look critically at the notions I had about myself, then compare them to the truth of God's Word. If they were in contradiction, I must reject them as false. For many, this process is lengthy, requiring discipline and faith. As I began reading Verna Birkey's book *You Are Very Special*, I was amazed at the chapter titles: "You Are Deeply Loved," "You Are a Person of Value," etc. In her book, she systematically took me through the Scripture to support these concepts that were so revolutionary to me. When thoughts came to me about being unlovable in God's eyes, the truth of His Word would ring in my heart: "Yes, I have loved you with an everlasting love" (Jer. 31:3). Ephesians 4:23 tells us we must "be renewed in the spirit of [our] mind."

I have concluded that many of the false notions we have are really lies planted by the enemy. Recently I was able to share this concept with a young woman named Tina from the midwest. She had called me because of her struggle with her emotions.

She said, "Jan, I'm really having trouble with my anger, and it's getting worse—not better. I'm angry at my kids and at my husband. I tell myself it's not right to be angry, but it does no good. What can I do?"

"Tina," I said, "let me share something with you that the Lord has been teaching me. Are you familiar with the parable of the wheat and the tares in Matthew 13:24-30?"

"Yes, a little," she replied.

"It's a beautiful illustration of what happens to us as victims," I continued. "The Scripture says that a man sowed good seed in his field, but while he slept the enemy came and sowed weeds among the wheat. When the wheat sprouted, so did the weeds.

"The servants of the man who owned the field went to their master and asked how the weeds got there when he had sown wheat. He replied, 'An enemy has done this.' They asked if they should pull up the weeds and the master said no. He explained that if they attempted to gather up the weeds, they might accidentally root up the wheat as well. He told them to wait until both had grown up and matured, until it was harvest time. At that time he would send out the harvesters to gather the weeds first, and bundle them and burn them. Then they could gather the wheat into his barn.

"I've found, Tina, that our childhood is very much like fertile ground. Many times there are those who plant good seed in our lives while we are children. For me it was my grandmother. However, since that ground is fertile, the enemy, often unbeknown to us, comes in and plants seeds of untruth in our hearts. Is this making sense to you?"

"Yes, it is," Tina replied.

"Those lies become deeply rooted in our lives and they

grow up and mature with us. The problem is that for many of us those lies become so ingrained we view them as truth. That is why the Scripture refers to the enemy—Satan—as the 'father of lies.' Can you think of some lies he has planted in your heart?"

"I'm not sure," Tina said thoughtfully, "but I do know I have trouble trusting God."

"Okay," I said, "let's look at that. Probably something happened in your childhood, whether it was a molestation or some other stressful event, that Satan could use, and he planted within your little child's heart the lie that said, *God is not trustworthy*. As that seed germinated and grew throughout your growing-up years, the enemy continued to reinforce the lie. He also might have put such thoughts in your head as, *If God really cares, why did He allow this to happen?* Other lies also could have included: *I'm a bad girl; I'm damaged goods; I have to be perfect in order to merit God's love; I'm unlovable; there's no hope for me.* All of these lies are planted by the enemy to affect our fruitfulness for God. They need to be exposed, rooted out and replaced with the truth of God's Word."

"Does that mean that my feelings are a lie and I should be denying them or standing against them?" Tina asked.

"Yes and no," I said. "The feelings are real, and need to be identified and worked through, but it will be helpful to realize that many times feelings are based on lies. If, for example, the enemy has planted a lie in my heart that says, *I am a bad girl and God does not love bad girls*, and if I believe that lie even on a subconscious level, it can evoke in me all kinds of feelings ranging from depression to guilt, to anger, to feelings of suicide. The truth is that I am loved by God, and I was chosen by Him from the foundation of the world. The Scripture says I am 'accepted in the beloved.' Therefore, what I must do first is recognize and expose the lie, and begin the process of rooting it out with the help of the Holy Spirit. Then I must replace that lie with the truth of God's Word. Do you understand what I'm getting at, Tina?"

"Yes, I really do. It's making a lot of sense to me. So now, I must ask the Holy Spirit to help me expose the lies and root them out in order to replace them ultimately with truth," Tina said with assurance.

"Yes. That last part is what the Scripture calls renewing your mind," I affirmed. "But remember: It's a process, and it takes time. The enemy will not give up easily."

The steps of rejecting false notions and renewing our minds go hand in hand. In psychological terms, this process is known as cognitive restructuring. It was coined by Dr. Albert Ellis, the founder of Rational-Emotive Therapy. According to his theory, a primary objective in therapy is to "help the client get free of illogical ideas and learn to substitute logical ideas in their place."[4] It is difficult to reject false notions and expect them to disappear if we do not replace them with the truth.

The Scripture is clear about this concept of renewing. Romans 12:2 says you are to be "transformed by the renewing of your mind." I began memorizing Scripture that talked about my importance to God. Isaiah 43 was a portion of Scripture that deeply ministered to me: "Fear not, for I have redeemed you;/ I have called you by your name;/ You are Mine" (v. 1). As I rehearsed these truths daily, I saw a difference in my life.

I was beginning to value myself as I was valued by God. This changed many of my relationships as well. Jesus said we are to love our neighbors as we love ourselves, but we cannot love our neighbors if we do not have an adequate healthy love for ourselves. The only sound foundation for our self-image comes from the truth of God's Word. We cannot conjure up self-image; it must be something we appropriate from His truth.

Picture a large, clear vase about half full of dark, murky water. Your job is to fill the vase with clean, fresh water until it no longer appears cloudy and dirty, and you have only an eyedropper to do it with. After the first few drops, you can see *no* significant change. Don't give up! Little by little, drop by drop, you continue to add the clean water. Eventually you will begin to see a difference. The water inside the vase is a little less dingy. The more water you add, the cleaner the water becomes. While there will be residual effects, you have made significant improvements. This is much like the process we must use as victims of incest and other wounds that make our self-image murky. As we incorporate the clear truth of God's Word, the false notions of the enemy that have corrupted our vessel begin to disseminate.

Distortions about God

In addition to renewing my mind with Scripture which focused on my self-concept, I realized I also needed a new concept of God. I had transferred many of my earthly father's characteristics to my heavenly Father, and these needed to be changed. As I look back, I am acutely aware of God's intervention and His perfect timing!

I had looked at God as a critical parent, assuming that He was never quite satisfied with my effort and that He was watching, waiting just to trip me up. When I failed in some way, I dreaded the punishment that I knew would come. I had difficulty accepting God's forgiveness and was convinced that I had to pay some type of penance first. After I sinned, I would walk around for days with a load of guilt, unable to accept the completeness of Christ's work on the cross.

During this period of time, three particular Bible verses were helpful. The first one, Nahum 1:7, says: "The LORD is good, a strong hold in the day of trouble; and he knoweth them that trust in him" (KJV). The other verses are Ecclesiastes 7:13 and 14: "Consider the work of God: for who can make that straight, which he hath made crooked? In the day of prosperity be joyful, but in the day of adversity consider: God also hath set the one over against the other, to the end that man should find nothing after him" (KJV).

For the first time I began to see my Lord as a good God who could use even the adversity I had experienced as a means of balancing my life. This was a difficult position for me to reach. I had been angry with God for not intervening in my life and had held Him accountable for years. Finally I realized that God had not orchestrated the molestation. Rather, His father's heart was grieved over the way that another's sin had so polluted my life. But He is a God who is able to redeem that which has been lost.

Restoring Right Relationships

We have discussed the concepts of rejecting false notions and renewing our minds. The next step toward rebuilding is restoring right relationships. Due to my many false notions about God, myself, and others, I lacked the ability to have meaningful, intimate relationships, holding back for fear of rejection. It became necessary for me to restore communication and develop new and healthier patterns of relating. When I started this restoration process, the one I dealt with was my relationship with God. As I opened myself up to Him and yielded to His will, I began to see significant changes in my other relationships. But sometimes it took sheer discipline and obedience.

Regarding my habit of being overly critical with my husband, sometimes I had to bite my tongue to avoid spilling out those critical thoughts. This had a great deal to do with my self-talk. If I focused on my husband's inadequacies throughout the day, it seemed that I was ready to pounce on him about something the moment he came home at night. If, however, I spent the day thanking the Lord for my husband's faithfulness, love and loyalty, I was much less prone to be critical. That is what Jesus meant when he said, "Out of the abundance of the heart the mouth speaks" (Matt. 12:34).

The restoration of relationships is an ongoing process for me. The Lord continues to show me additional areas that need His healing touch in my relationships with my parents, my daughters, my husband, my Lord, myself, and with others. The task of rebuilding is not easy but it can be done. As I mentioned in chapter 7, soon after I completed therapy, I attended a seminar at our church, conducted by Dr. Betty Coble Lawther entitled "Woman, Aware and Choosing." The seminar is designed to enhance a woman's self-esteem so that she can be all that she was intended to be. In the first session, Betty challenged us to write down twenty characteristics we like about ourselves. That first night I could barely come up with three. Through the ten-week course, Betty encouraged us to "build upon our strengths" and not to focus on our weaknesses. As I incorporated her ideas, my husband saw the change and our relationship grew steadily.

Betty also talked about our role as adult daughters. This helped me to approach my relationship with my parents from the proper perspective. I am an adult woman who, as their daughter, continues to honor their position. But I am no longer subject to their authority in my life. This is a key issue. Many victims find themselves relating to their parents as they did when they were children. This often comes from a deep hunger for love they never received. It is important that victims change this pattern and not continue to revert to the child position when relating to their parents. If this is not done, the woman will never reach the emotional maturity that is necessary to maintain healthy adult relationships. As we discussed previously, the woman must take up for her child within, and not expect others to nurture her, when in reality, others are unable or unwilling to do so.

Inner Healing

I became aware that in this area of restoration there was an entire spiritual sphere of my being that had not yet been healed. I prayed that the Lord would show me what was missing. Several months went by and though I was growing and learning spiritually, I still sensed I needed something more.

I knew Lana Bateman had a ministry of inner healing in Dallas, Texas, but because I had gone through extensive healing already, I was skeptical when a friend urged me to go through the inner healing prayer. Lana's ministry, known as Philippian Ministries, requires you to go through several steps prior to making an appointment. One of these steps is to read Lana's book *God's Crippled Children*.[5] The second step is to examine your motives for the inner healing and to have a true desire to put away all that stands between you and a deeper relationship with God. While I was reading the book, I felt the need for this healing in my life, and within a few months, through God's leading, made an appointment with Lana. During our time together, I gained new insights and found freedom from bondages that had held me captive.

Lana prayed with me and we went through my entire life. We focused our prayers on many other hurtful events as well as the molestation. One of these was an experience I had as a five year old in kindergarten. I wet my pants during story time and left a big puddle on the floor. The teacher asked who was responsible and the entire class called out my name. I was horrified and embarrassed. The teacher made me get several paper towels and wipe up the floor. As I shared this painful memory with Lana, she recognized the deep hurt and anger that I had as a child. It was apparent that the anger I felt then had never been released. Lana helped me to visualize the Lord Jesus with me in that situation, down on His knees helping me clean up my mess. She urged me in the prayer to ask and to give forgiveness to this teacher who had hurt me so deeply. I was then able to release the anger and embarrassment that I had hidden away for all those years.

The inner healing prayer stresses the Lord Jesus' presence with us from the foundation of the world. As Lana prayed with me through my life, she continually used the phrase, "He was there." That phrase still echoes comfort in my heart. Knowing that I have been His from the foundation of the world, I'm able to experience God and His love for me in a deeper, more intimate way.

Not too long ago as I poured out my heart to God, I told Him that even though I'd made significant spiritual progress and much inner healing had taken place, I still didn't know Him as a father in a healthy way. I simply asked, "Lord, show me your father's heart." I'm not sure how many days passed before the answer came. I was sitting in our den reading one evening when I looked up and observed my two little girls and their daddy in the living room in front of the television. Heather took two pillows from her room and placed one under her dad's head and the other beside him where she laid down. Kellie, my two year old, picked up her favorite blanket and placed it on her dad's chest where she proceeded to rest her head. Don glanced my way with a tender smile on his face as if to say, "These are *my* girls." In the instant following that glance, my heavenly Father whispered so sweetly in my heart, "*That* is my father's heart for you, Jan."

Fighting the Battle

We have discussed at some length the rebuilding of the self-image and of relationships. It is important to realize that this step is a continual progression. I don't believe I will ever be able to say, "I have fully arrived!" But I am confident that God will continue to show me areas in which growth is needed or a battle may have to be fought.

I am reminded again of Nehemiah. In chapter 4 we read

that there were those who opposed building up the wall in Jerusalem. Nehemiah's adversaries were so opposed that they took up weapons against the workers in trying to discourage them from building. In verse 17 we read: "Those who built on the wall, and those who carried burdens, loaded themselves so that with one hand they worked at construction, and with the other held a weapon." We must realize that the rebuilding of our self-image and our relationships is opposed by the enemy, Satan. He wants to keep us bound by our past and thus keep us ineffective for the kingdom of God. Like Nehemiah and his workers, we must be diligent in the work of rebuilding. We, too, can expect attacks from the enemy, so we must equip ourselves with our sword, the Word of God. With assurance, we can say as Nehemiah did in verse 20, "Our God will fight for us."

Josh McDowell shares an analogy that is so appropriate in *His Image . . . My Image*. He writes:

> We're like a circus elephant tied down by a bicycle chain. We ask how one small chain could hold a powerful elephant. The trainer explains that the chain doesn't hold him; it's the elephant's memory that keeps him from trying to escape.

> When the elephant was very young, he didn't have the strength to break the chain or pull free. He learned then that the chain was stronger than he was and he hasn't forgotten that. The result is that the elephant, now full-grown and powerful, remembers only that he tried to break the chain and couldn't. So he never tries again. His memory, not the chain, binds him. Of course, occasionally an elephant does discover he can break the chain, and from then on his keeper has trouble controlling him.[6]

Our self-image is much like that. But we *can* break free by rejecting false notions, renewing our minds and restoring our relationships!

With your weapon in hand . . . build on!

PRACTICAL INSIGHTS

1. In *His Image ... My Image*, Josh McDowell states our self-image is made up of 3 vital components:

    - a sense of belonging;
    - a sense of worthiness;
    - a sense of competence.[7]

    Divide a sheet of paper into those three categories. List specific times and ways in which you feel a sense of belonging, worth or competence. Notice if one of those columns tends to outweigh the others. If your competence list is longer, you may be one who "performs" in order to get love. If your "belonging" list outweighs the others, you may be a "joiner," one who needs to be involved with others to gain acceptance. If your "worthy" list outweighs the others, check on the defenses you've constructed in an attempt to ward off the feeling of unworthiness. Ideally, these three areas need to be in balance. (Remember all things are possible with God!)

2. Read Isaiah 43, and *His Image ... My Image* by Josh McDowell. Plan within the next six months to complete a Bible study on self-esteem and the attributes of God. Ask the Holy Spirit to help you reject the faulty notions you have about yourself and about Him, and to replace those with the truth of His Word.

3. Memorize 2 Corinthians 10:5.

CHAPTER 11

Step X:

Express Concern and Empathize with Others

After appearing on a Christian talk show, I received more than a hundred letters from across the country. Many of those letters expressed a desire to help others, as demonstrated by the following:

Dear Jan,

Thank you very much for reaching out. I hope one day, when I'm healed, I can help others who have been hurt and victimized to recover from their pains too. I'm seeing more and more how many people are hurting, are in pain, and need a compassionate heart to turn to. Thank you for the love and care you have for me and many other women like me. With great appreciation and thanksgiving.

Gratefully,

Lydia

Helping Others

Many women have an interest in helping others. For most, there is a compelling need to bring value out of the valueless tragedies of their own lives. In many ways, helping others provides an opportunity to use what has been destructive in a constructive way. You do this on a daily basis. For instance, a coworker comes into work late, grumbling and complaining of the mishaps with his car, and you share similar experiences in an attempt to say, "Hey, I've been there too. Believe me, it will work out!"

This principle is primarily outlined in 2 Corinthians 1:3-4:

> Blessed be the God and Father of our Lord Jesus Christ, the Father of mercies and God of all comfort, who comforts us in all our tribulation, that we may be able to comfort those who are in any trouble, with the comfort with which we ourselves are comforted by God.

God never intended for us to be a sponge! We are not to soak up His comforts and mercies to build a reservoir, but in order that we can ultimately release them in someone's life. Some of you may ask, "Aren't you robbing the other person of receiving God's comfort by intervening?" Absolutely not! We are His channels of comfort, just as we are to be salt and light in this world. The idea in the Greek is that we are to invoke or implement comfort and exhortation in the lives of others. How good of God to work in us a comfort that is reusable!

For me, there's nothing like sharing with a person who has been where I am and has successfully overcome the problem. I think of the time when our daughter, Heather, turned two and graduated from the crib to a bed. *That was the week that was!* In a five-day period, she got into more mischief than I ever imagined possible for our nearly angelic child! During her nap time, she emptied her entire dresser of clothing and decorated the room. On the second day, she found the baby powder and sprinkled her clothes, her bed and the room. After disciplining her, I wrote these two days off as her experimentation with freedom. By the third day I had reached my limit. Not only did she take her clothing out of the dresser, but she managed to get a hold of some baby oil and doused her bed and room within minutes of my putting her down for her nap. I finally did what most harried mothers of preschoolers do — I called a friend. My friend Mae, whose daughter is a year older than Heather, assured me that "this too will pass." When she shared some similar catastrophes that she had weathered the year before, I realized that I, too, could make it through the terrible twos. I needed her. We all need each other. I am not so sure that "misery loves company," but I know misery loves to know a person who has been there and made it through successfully.

Expressing concern and empathizing with others provides hope. Empathizing with others also brings continued healing to the comforter. As I share my personal experience with women, I am awed by the grace of God. God is the only one who can cause *all* things to work together for good in the lives of those "who are the called according to His purpose" (Rom. 8:28). Each time I am privileged to share my testimony, it is as if my heavenly Father is rubbing a healing ointment over my scar. Many times I have been challenged by well-meaning Christians who say, "If you really have been healed, this scar would disappear." I respond in two ways. First, I explain that I may never reach complete healing in this life even though God has done tremendous miracles in my life. God continues to show me areas that need His healing touch as a result of my childhood experiences. Second, I tell the person that I am reminded of Christ's appearance to the disciples after the resurrection. Have you ever wondered why the scars on Jesus's hands, feet and side remain even in His glorified body? Could we dare accuse Him that His body is not whole and perfect because the scars remain? I think not. I believe His scars remain, not so much as a reminder to Himself (How could He forget what He had endured in our place?) but for the benefit of those around Him. The scars are there for every Thomas and for every unbelief. For those who doubt Christ's ability to identify with their pain, and for those who preach only prosperity and health. It is for them—for us—that His scars remain.

The same principle holds true for us. He allows us to carry with us the scars of our lives. What we do with those scars is what is important. We can draw attention to ourselves and continually open up the scar and lament our tragedies of life, or we can point to the scar as a means of identity, thank God for the healing that has taken place, and encourage others to trust God for healing in their own circumstances. This is what Paul talks about in 2 Corinthians 1:3-4—comforting others with the comfort we have received from God.

Ezekiel 36:34-36 speaks about this restoration and healing. Verse 35 says, "This land that was desolate has become like the garden of Eden." Who but God could take the devastation of a life and cause fruit to be found therein? I am utterly amazed at His work in my heart and life. He has taken the emptiness of a tragic event and brought forth fruit that has been made manifest in the lives of others. I have shared my story with hundreds of women, and some have asked me, "Was it worth it? Would you change your past if you could?" That is a difficult question to answer. I am not sure what I would do, but I know this: God has truly restored to me "the years that the swarming locust has eaten" (Joel 2:25), and I have been reminded that "everyone to whom much is given, from him much will be required" (Luke 12:48). A friend once said, "Jan, you've been given much heartache and healing. You have much to share with those who need to hear."

Supporting Group Ministry

What is the best way to begin to minister to others? Most women who ask this have a desire to set up support groups in their church or to speak on this subject. I encourage them to be available on a one-to-one basis before starting a group ministry. My own ministry began when God brought women to me through a Bible study and I learned how to be faithful in small areas. As I look back now, I realize how premature it was for me to begin that first support group at my church. I still had so much growing and healing ahead of me, but God was gracious and allowed me to be a part of a unique healing experience. The support group environment is one of the most rewarding and instrumental tools in the healing process for victims. I have co-led numerous groups and have been privileged to see God working miracles in the lives of many women, and He uses the support group to further my own healing. Many times women in my group ask me, "How many groups do I *have* to go through?" I encourage them by telling them I have been through several and I am still gaining new insights.

Before any individual—lay person or professional—leads a support group, she needs to carefully examine three areas: leadership, goals, and guidelines.

Leadership

Leadership is a key factor in the success of our groups. The combination of a professional and a lay person, preferably a "recovered victim," acting as co-leaders is a dynamic pair. The professional provides a special stability, security, and objectivity for the group. The recovered victim provides hope and can relate to the women in a positive and subjective way.

Other combinations will work successfully, but I have found that the combined professional and lay person provide a positive, balanced environment in which healing is promoted. Each has certain advantages. If the professional is a male, he must have a great reservoir of knowledge in the area of incest and an ability to empathize with the women at a deep level. Since many victims come from dysfunctional homes, the combination of male/female leaders provides a unique opportunity to work out unresolved issues stemming from their family origin. If the professional is a female working with a female co-leader, I believe it is important that one of them be a motherly figure. Most victims have difficulty relating to their mothers and it is helpful if the group can address this issue. The leadership factor seems to be the cornerstone of a successful group. It is not always necessary to have a professional directly involved, but one should be available in an advisory capacity.

One such group started as a result of a small workshop I conducted in a quaint little town in central California. Marlene, one of the women who attended, had never been victimized but she had a genuine love and concern for her friend Celia, who had been abused as a child. I counseled Celia and Marlene after the workshop and encouraged Marlene just to be a support to those God brought her way. Before she knew it, God opened the doors for her to begin a small support group in her home church. Marlene contacted me, and over the phone we discussed the framework and goals. She has the help of a local professional who acts as an advisor, but Marlene holds the group on her own. She calls me at times with questions and praise reports. Marlene often feels inadequate to comfort and guide the six women the Lord has brought to her, yet God continues to give her wisdom because she is an available vessel to Him.

Goals

Once the leadership has been established, defining the goals of the group is imperative. Goals may differ from group to group and depend to some extent upon the leaders and their respective positions, but the following goals are essential:

1.   Provide an environment where women can feel safe to express themselves and where acceptance and unconditional love are demonstrated.

2.   Provide accurate information about victimization and the by-products that result.

3.   Provide a place where hope is instilled.

4.   Provide an environment where new behaviors can be tested and faulty beliefs challenged.

5.   Provide a warm, caring atmosphere where members will experience the true nature of God and His love for them.

Other specific goals may need to be discussed and implemented, depending upon the prospective group members. Specific goals are often *present-oriented* in that they deal with the here-and-now, yet should be viewed from their relevance to the victim's past. If, for example, Joan enters the group with the specific goal of developing a deeper level of intimacy with her husband, we first address the difficulty she has with intimacy and where the difficulty originated. After we have laid the groundwork of where the problem comes from, we discuss how the difficulty is maintained by Joan through her thoughts and actions. Then we set about to challenge some of Joan's unrealistic beliefs about intimacy and encourage her to begin behaving differently. All of this, of course, takes time and is a very individualized process. The main point I would like to emphasize is that the specific goals related to the here-and-now problems must be seen from a historical viewpoint in order for lasting change to occur. Some professionals may disagree with me on this point; however, I believe the combination of both insight and action are essential for the victim's recovery.

Guidelines
Finally, after the leadership has been established and goals are set, some specific guidelines are in order. Guidelines should include practical issues such as (1) time schedule, (2) number of members, (3) screening criteria, (4) confidentiality, (5) the

framework of the meetings, (6) the cost, (7) where the group is to meet, and (8) how the group is to be formed. These depend upon who is conducting the support group, and upon the location, i.e., if it is being held in a church, for example.

We have found it favorable to have our group run for ten weeks, with a maximum of ten women, meeting once a week for ninety minutes. It seems women can commit themselves to a ten-week period without feeling they have over-committed. At the same time, we do not guarantee them that they will be all "fine and dandy" at the end of ten weeks. Rather, we help them realize it sometimes takes two or three ten-week sessions before they will see real progress.

The screening process is very important in the overall success of the group. We pay special attention to potential participants, spend time in prayerful consideration and seek professional expertise in determining group membership.

For the group to function well, it is necessary for members to be at different levels in the healing process. Some may have worked through many issues in private therapy, while others are at the beginning stages of understanding victimization and its impact. I spend considerable time asking each potential member about her history, her previous therapy experience, whether she has been or is suicidal and what type of support system exists around her.

As with all groups of this nature, confidentiality is imperative and should be guaranteed and strictly adhered to by all. If the support group is within the church, special consideration must be given to how the group is formed, whether it is advertised in the church bulletin and whether group members are assured that their identities will be protected. Furthermore, each member of the group agrees to confidentiality on all details within the group session. This must be maintained in relation to other members *and* to their own spouses, thus affording protection for each individual member.

Express Concern and Empathize with Others

As to the framework for the group meetings, we use the ten steps, FREE TO CARE, as presented in this book. This is not to say that we address each step consecutively each week. Quite the contrary is true. We allow the women to experience the group according to their particular needs and gently guide and direct them into and through each central issue (the ten steps) as necessary for their healing. Different groups address some of the foundation issues repeatedly. God has continued to confirm to me that He authored the FREE TO CARE concept.

Honoring Him
Although there is value in sharing our experiences in order to provide comfort and healing for others, I believe the highest goal of expressing concern and empathizing with others is to bring glory to God. In Ezekiel 36:36 we read: "Then the nations which are left all around you shall know that I, the LORD, have rebuilt the ruined places and planted what was desolate. I, the LORD, have spoken it, and I will do it." When we share with others the healing we have experienced through God's intervention in our lives, we glorify Him.

I think of Joseph in the Old Testament. Although Joseph was victimized by others, and I'm sure there were times when he cried out to God to intervene, still he allowed God to reign sovereign in his life and later reaped the benefits of a yielded life. I do not believe Joseph's misfortunes were directed by God, but I do believe God took the brokenness of Joseph's life and the circumstances and caused them to work for good in the lives of many around him — including his immediate family.

There were many times in the process of my healing that I cried out my complaints before God. One such time involved my two little girls. One August evening, Kellie, who was eighteen months old at the time, became extremely ill. She had a fever of 104°F, and was vomiting so frequently and severely

161

that she could not breathe at times. In my panic and fear I cried, "Lord, I would intervene instantly for my child if I had the power—so why don't You intervene in the lives of Your children? If Your love is supposed to be greater than mine, how can You stand by and do nothing?" The question remained unanswered as we rushed Kellie to the emergency room that evening.

The following day when Heather, four, was playing in the front yard, she fell and cut her chin. Heather ran into the house bloody and scared. As I tried to comfort her, I felt panic again. "Lord," I cried from the child within me, "why don't You intervene? Don't You care what happens to Your children?" No answer came.

Two and a half weeks passed. I was sitting in my living room watching my little girls playing and giggling together on the floor. As I watched them enjoying each other and their renewed health, His answer came.

"Jan," the Lord whispered gently, "I see the end from the beginning."

He saw what I could not see. He knew my girls would be healthy again. He knew that in my life, restoration would take place. He knew about the hope for recovery that would be instilled in the lives of many victims with whom I have shared. He sees the end from the beginning. He sees in your life what you cannot see.

You can trust Him. I know. His promise in Isaiah 49:15-16 is true for you today:

> Can a woman forget her nursing child, that she should not have compassion on the son of her womb? Yes, they may forget, yet will I not forget you. Behold, I have indelibly imprinted [tattooed] a picture of you on the palm of each of My hands. O [your name], your walls are continually before Me. (Amplified version)

There is no situation in our lives that God is not able to

redeem if we are willing to place it all in His hands. If we allow God to work His healing in our lives and submit ourselves to ministering to others according to His timing, we will receive manifold blessings and God will be honored. God does the impossible. He is the only one who can take the vessel that has been marred and rework it gently on His potter's wheel to become a vessel unto honor.

God is willing to use us if we are obedient and available. I received a letter just before Christmas one year that confirmed God's desire to comfort others through the comfort we have received:

> Dearest Jan,
>
> Since I received your tape a few months ago, I have to say what a change! I have dealt with things that all my life I didn t understand about myself. A couple of months ago, I rented a room out in my home . . . a young woman moved in and she wasn't here a week before it became apparent that she, too, was an incest victim. My sister ended up moving in as well and so now there are three victims living in my home. I don't have all the answers, but thanks to you I have some. My plan is to someday be able to fully commit myself to other victims, but for now, I will work with the three I have!
>
> God bless you,
>
> Maria

We have now looked at the entire FREE TO CARE process.

First of all, we examined the need to face the problem by examining ourselves realistically. Then we discussed the importance of recounting the incident and experiencing the feelings involved with a therapist or knowledgeable support person—surveying the damage and loss in order that we can intelligently rebuild. We outlined the crucial step of establishing the responsibility of the aggressor and any co-contributors. We saw the advantages of tracing behavioral difficulties and symptoms, and of observing others and educating ourselves. We detailed the prerequisites of confronting the aggressor: Presenting the issues face to face, having a goal of reconciliation, confronting from a position of strength, and having an organized format in mind before facing the aggressor. We looked at acknowledging forgiveness as a four-fold process, and we identified the vital step of rebuilding our self-image and our relationships through rejecting false notions and renewing our mind. Finally, we concluded by exploring the advantages of expressing concern and empathizing with others, and by considering the necessary ingredients for a support group ministry.

There is one final area that must be addressed. It is an area I had no intention of covering when I began writing this book. However, it reveals the completion of the work the Holy Spirit intended in the process of my healing. It is the final chapter: "Restoration—His Redeeming Work."

PRACTICAL INSIGHTS

1. Be open to the Holy Spirit. Ask Him to send you one person whom you might encourage along this healing process. Remember, God does not require that you have it all together before you can reach out to someone who is hurting. He only asks that you comfort them with the comfort He gave to you. Record the number of times in a week you have been given the opportunity to encourage someone else. Praise the Lord for His answer!

2. Read Isaiah 40. He will renew your strength as you wait on Him.

3. Memorize Isaiah 50:4 and 2 Corinthians 1:3-4.

CHAPTER 12

Restoration — His Redeeming Work

Gideon. Gideon. Read about Gideon." The thought flashed through my mind, over and over. By the third day, I could no longer escape from the compelling phrase. I sat down in the study and opened my Bible to Judges, chapter 6. I read the account of Gideon—his call, his fleeces, his victory. As I re-read verses 25 and 26, I stopped. I was moved deep within as the Holy Spirit spoke to me through these two verses. I prayed, "Lord, show me what significance these words have in my life."

I read and reread:

> Now it came to pass the same night that the LORD said to him [Gideon], "Take your father's young bull, the second bull of seven years old, *and tear down the altar of Baal that your father has, and cut down the wooden image that is beside it;* and build an altar to the LORD your God on top of this rock in the proper arrangement, and take the second bull and offer a burnt sacrifice *with the wood of the image which you shall cut down* (emphasis mine).

The Holy Spirit impressed me with a notion that was hard for me to hear as He showed me something significant in the life of Gideon. The Lord knew Gideon would lead His people into great victory over the Midianites. But before He commissioned Gideon to perform the task, God directed him to take care of some "family business." Gideon was told to go out and tear down the idol of Baal that his father had constructed. In its place, Gideon was to build an altar to the Lord, he was to sacrifice an acceptable bull, using the wood from the idol as the means by which the bull would be consumed.

As I sat on my couch that morning, tears flowed down my face. In a tender way, the Spirit seemed to be saying, "Jan, you have some 'family business' to take care of."

I wrestled within. "Lord, what do these two verses have to do with me?"

Gently, He seemed to speak in the depths of my soul, "Jan, you need to take down the sin of your stepfather and replace it with an altar."

As I looked at those verses, over and over, it became clearer. Gideon had taken the very sin of his father, represented by the wood of the image, and placed it on an altar, under a sacrifice, offering it in an acceptable manner that honored the Lord.

The Holy Spirit showed me that Gideon could have focused on his father's sin. He no doubt was grieved daily as he confronted the idol of Baal near his father's house. For me it had been easy to focus on the sin of my stepfather. Daily I was faced with some of the effects of his sin in my life. But God instructed Gideon to take the wood of the image and place it *under* the sacrifice. In essence, he was to take his focus off the sin and put it on the sacrifice. The Holy Spirit revealed to me that I, too, had been concentrating on the sin. I was to take the sin of my stepfather and place it on the altar, *under* the sacrifice, no longer focusing on the sin but totally on the sacrifice.

But there was something more. The Holy Spirit seemed to say, "Gideon's offering of sacrifice was not for his father only but also for himself." He sacrificed the bull for *both* of them and their sins. With a jolt, the truth hit me. Jesus was the Sacrifice, and in light of His death on the cross, there was no difference between my stepfather and me. We both stand in the shadow of that cross, not as victim and victimizer, but as one in Him—both in need of forgiveness, both in need of Jesus' shed blood that cleanses us from all sin. One simple truth brought clarity to my struggle—*Jesus paid it all.* I wept as the truth sank deep within a heart that knew more of justice and judgment than of mercy and grace. As I ended that prayer time, I asked the Lord to show me clearly what I needed to do.

Later that afternoon I called Pam, a friend who has a wonderful ministry of intercession. In the course of our conversation, I told Pam that I had been unable to work on my manuscript for days because something was missing but I had no idea what it was.

Almost before I got those words out, Pam said, "Jan, I've been interceding for you for three days. I've sensed in my spirit that the Lord wants to deal with you about some issues with your parents." She continued, "The Lord has laid some things on my heart for you, but they're going to be difficult for you to hear."

Knowing Pam's sensitivity, I said, "Please share them with me."

Pam spoke gently, "Jan, I've sensed that there is still a spirit of judgment in your heart against your parents. It's this very spirit that is binding God's ability to work in your parents' lives. Your pride is interfering. You're not able to finish the manuscript because the final chapter hasn't yet happened."

Immediately, I felt an inner confirmation. What Pam was saying was true! Although I had experienced restoration in my life, it had not taken place fully in my parents' lives. Something was holding them back. I'd confronted my parents and worked through the steps of forgiveness, but the Holy Spirit was showing me I needed to go a level deeper.

"Pam," I cried, "if this is true, what should I do?"

Quietly, confidently, she told me. "You need to go to your

parents and ask for their forgiveness for the spirit of judgment that you've held against them."

"But how can I do that?" I argued. "Won't that invalidate everything that has taken place so far?"

In her reassuring way, Pam said, "It is not an invalidation of the steps you've already taken; it is a *completion*.

Suddenly, it all made sense to me. The story of Gideon took on more personal meaning. The Lord wanted me to bridge the gap, to face the fact that my stepfather and mother were not the culprits of a devastating series of events in my life, but were themselves victims and tools used by the enemy. The Scripture says the enemy's goal is to "steal, and to kill, and to destroy" (John 10:10). I realized Satan had initiated the events of my childhood and his goal was to destroy not only me but also my parents. Yes, my parents had accountability and they had made choices that were destructive, but so had I.

For the first time I saw the totality of what Christ accomplished on the cross. I saw a glimpse of a deep truth from an eternal perspective. There was a part of me that my stepfather could not touch. The Scriptures call it our "inner man"—our "spirit man." It is the part of us that is "graven on the palms of God's hands" from the foundation of the world. In the realm of the spirit, no earthly event has the power to touch what the Father holds in His hand. It is that inner man, the spirit within, that has brought life out of death in my life. It is the power of the cross. It is the redeeming work of His shed blood that allows us to fellowship in His suffering and experience the power of the resurrection, even in this earthly life.

As I ended my conversation with Pam that day, I asked her to continue to pray for me. I didn't want to act without God completing the work in the depths of my heart. I didn't want to go to my parents without a genuine sincerity and conviction. I vacillated for days. I struggled as I thought about the hundreds of victims who might read this chapter and simply try to apply this step, foregoing all the previous ones. I prayed and asked the Lord to show me His heart in this matter as I committed myself to walk in obedience — regardless of the cost. I asked Him to confirm His way through His Word.

Later that week I was led to three Scripture passages that I knew well. The first was 1 John 1:7: "But if we walk in the light as He is in the light, we have fellowship with one another, and the blood of Jesus Christ His Son cleanses us from all sin."

The second was one verse pointing out the completeness of His work on the cross. Colossians 1:14: "In whom we have redemption [been set free] through His blood, the forgiveness of sins." The third passage was more specific, and it cut to my heart. It was 2 Corinthians 2:5-11, especially verses 7 and 8 which said: "So that, on the contrary, you ought rather to *forgive* and *comfort* him, lest perhaps such a one be swallowed up [utterly discouraged] with too much sorrow. Therefore I urge you to *reaffirm* [give evidence of] your love to him" (emphasis mine). I could not refute the groundwork the Holy Spirit was laying. He was preparing my heart in order that I might walk in obedience.

After I pondered my course of action for several days, the Lord did something unusual. One evening I could not fall asleep. It seemed as though the Holy Spirit was saying, "Get up, Jan, there's something I have for you." I found myself at my desk with pen in hand and yellow pad before me. The words flowed easily as a poem emerged before my eyes. I had not written a poem of any significance for fifteen years, but as I wrote, the tears flowed and the message was straight from the heart. I knew this was the expression that God was going to use in relation to my parents.

A few more days went by. Finally I was ready to share with my parents what God had so tenderly worked in my heart. I called my parents and arranged a time to visit. My grandfather, who had recently come to live with them, had been wanting me to take some pictures of him on his three-wheeled bicycle to send to relatives. I told my parents I was coming to do that.

As I drove to my parents' home, apprehension and nervousness set in. Questions plagued me. Was I doing the right thing? Would this act in someway diminish what had taken place three years earlier in the confrontation? Would the message conveyed really release my parents and allow for restoration? I frankly could not answer those questions. I did not know. But I did know amidst those uncertainties that God was leading me to obey Him, to lay down my sense of justice and judgment, and to be instead an extension of His mercy and grace.

I arrived at my parents' home in the early afternoon. When I arrived at the front door, Grandpa, who was ninety-eight years old, was eagerly awaiting my arrival. He was all decked out in his new shirt and trousers with his favorite red suspenders. A cap shielded his eyes from the sun. We visited awhile, then went back outside where I took Grandpa's picture. As he sat there smiling so proudly, I could not help but think that for each of us the day would hold a different significance.

As we walked back into the house, I turned to my mom and said, "I'd like to talk to you and Dad alone for a few minutes." I saw the look in her eye as she glanced briefly at my dad. The look I knew well. It was as if to say, "Oh, no. What now?"

As I sat down with them that warm, summer day, I could not hold back the tears. "Dad, Mom, I'm here today because there are some things I need to share with you." I told them the story of Gideon and of how I had come to realize that I held them under judgment. I handed them each a copy of the poem I had written, saying, "This best expresses what I want to say." I read it aloud.

Restoration — His Redeeming Work

Dearest Dad/Mom,

How many words passed between us
All through the silent years?
No words were ever spoken,
But, oh, the countless tears.
I've seen the depth of your pain,
In your eyes despair and grief.
I've gone before the Savior
And I've asked for your relief.
My gentle Shepherd showed me,
In, oh, so delicate a way
That I had not released you
From a debt you could not pay.
He whispered very softly
In a heart still plagued with pride,
"It is for this very reason
That I sent my Son who died."
Then Jesus brought me to His cross,
And said, "It's all been done.
I paid it all, so long ago
That in Me . . . you'd be one."
Dad, Mom, will you forgive me
For the judgment I've imposed?
And may we walk restored,
In the love that He's disclosed.
For Dad, Mom, it's only in the light
Of His mercy and His love,
That we can walk as His —
Forgiven — eternally above.

As I read, we wept together. After I finished reading, I choked out through the tears, "Will you please forgive me for the judgment I've held you under?"

171

The tears streaming from their eyes gave me the answer. At that moment, the spirit of judgment was broken. The enemy, Satan, could not hold captive what was paid for at the cross. How gracious and patient my Lord is with me. He did not hold me accountable for something I had not understood. His only requirement is that "we walk in the light as He is in the light," in order that "we have fellowship with one another, and the blood of Jesus Christ His Son cleanses us from all sin" (1 John 1:7).

Through his tears, my dad said, "Jan, I haven't sensed any bad feelings from you at all, but I have felt that something has been holding me back in my relationship with God. Jan, we love you."

I stood up and ran across the room and embraced them both. As the tears flowed, they seemed to be washing away the last speck of bitterness and judgment that remained in my heart.

I do not yet know the full impact of this step. But I do know the sense of freedom I experienced with my parents that day. I do know that "whatever you loose on earth will be loosed in heaven" (Matt. 18:18). I do know that with God all things are possible. I shared with my dad that day that I had visions of us ministering together one day, not as victim and victimizer, but as one in Him. Both forgiven. Both victorious. Jesus paid it all.

I pray as you read this final chapter you will see it in its proper perspective. The Lord brought me to this point five years after I acknowledged my need to resolve the issues of my past. He took me through the process, step by step. He has shown me the value of each step in the process and how one step tends to build upon the other. I don't contend that He will deal with you exactly as He has with me, but I invite you to examine the issues and the steps as they apply in your situation. *My challenge* to you is that you be willing to risk the pain and get to the root of the problem. *My caution* to you is that you do not prematurely apply the more "spiritual" steps in an effort to heal quickly. *My encouragement to you is that it's worth it!*

I am free today—FREE TO CARE for those whom I love most:

> My Lord,
>> my husband,
>>> my children,
>>>> my parents,
>>>>> myself.

He has done a wonderful work in my life. He can do the same for you.

For the LORD will comfort [insert your name],/ He will comfort all [your] waste places;/ He will make [your] wilderness like Eden,/ And [your] desert like the garden of the LORD;/ Joy and gladness will be found in it,/ Thanksgiving and the voice of melody. (Isa. 51:3).

The Lord never lost sight of that ten-year-old little girl who was wounded so long ago. He loved me then as He loves me now.

> *Jesus paid it all,*
>> *All to Him I owe.*
>> *Sin had left a crimson stain,*
>> *He washed it white as snow.*

No matter what deep hurt you have experienced, He is able to redeem it. If you will allow Jesus to walk with you through this FREE TO CARE process, He will take *your* valley of trouble and give you a *Door of Hope*.

Commonly Asked Questions about Sexual Abuse and Recovery

1. QUESTION: Is it *really* possible to repress such significant events as abuse from our past?

Although this remains a very controversial issue even among clinicians, I answer an unequivocal *yes* to this question, having experienced repression personally and having worked with many clients with repressed memory.

It is important to note here that repression for our purposes means *a blocking out or splitting off*. Most victims of repressed memories have small pieces of the total memory, but have blocked out the traumatic or confusing details in order to survive what they could not process or understand. I believe this is God's gracious mechanism to shield us *for a time* from whatever is too difficult to manage.

Most repressed victims have not obliterated the entire memory, but often have bits of the events preceding or subsequent to the traumatic memory. For instance, in my own life I had always remembered that around age five I had had a very serious nosebleed that required hospitalization. I can vividly see myself on my mother's yellow Chenille bedspread with our housekeeper trying to stop the profuse bleeding. I was bleeding from my nose and coughing up blood to such an extent that I had to be rushed to the emergency room to have my nose packed. Both my siblings and mother recalled this incident. I discovered, however, that the nosebleed was the subsequent memory to an incident that immediately preceded it. It was this memory that I had repressed for over thirty years. The full memory took approximately six years to return and came in little pieces over time. The Lord gently revealed what had really happened that summer day.

175

I had been warned on numerous occasions not to play in the alley behind our house, but on this particular day, I chose not to obey. While playing in the alley I was met by a teenage boy who forced me to have oral sex. The force of the ejaculation must have burst blood vessels which produced the severe bleeding. While running through the backyard I made a vow not to tell (or even remember), because I had been a *bad* girl by disobeying.

As the Lord eventually revealed this memory, it was through prayer that I made many discoveries. I realized that much of my Christian walk had been compulsive and I was often obsessed about *always* obeying and figuring out the right thing to do. I had set up an internal rule: *If I do the right thing and obey, I won't be hurt.* I had created my own source of protection that required complete and absolute obedience which, of course, was impossible to achieve. Through prayer, I eventually confessed my self-protection plan and asked Jesus to comfort the little girl part of me who had convinced herself she was bad. It was through the revelation of this memory that God was able to bring His healing balm to a place in my life that I had not even recognized needed healing. "If we had forgotten the name of our God,/ Or stretched out our hands to a foreign god,/ Would not God search this out?/ For He knows the secrets of the heart" (Ps. 44:20-21).

The remembering of this long-forgotten event brought new understanding into many areas of my life. The Lord showed me how this memory had locked inside a whole system of thinking, feeling and behaving that became my source of protection. I had been in bondage to a legalism that could not provide the love and safety I so desperately needed.

Through a simple prayer, I asked Jesus to comfort and bring healing to that little girl. I'll never forget how He prompted me to walk to the alley where I forgave the nameless face who had violated me that day. Then he moved me through the backyard where I surrendered to His care, abandoning my need to be perfect. Finally, I went into the house where He comforted the child who had asked her housekeeper if she was going to die. He brought with Him new life and redemption to a deep wound that had permeated my life, even though I was unaware of it.

When *Door of Hope* was written I described in Chapter Three an incident of sexual abuse perpetrated by my stepfather when I was ten years old. There were other memories which did not surface until later in my healing process, including the one described above. The abuse by my stepfather began at age seven and continued until I moved out of my parents home at twenty-one. I do not know to this day if I have other memories that have been repressed, but I do know that God is faithful to reveal what we need to know when we are ready to receive it. I continue to pray as David did in Psalm 139:23-24: "Search me, O God, and know my heart;/ Try me, and know my anxieties;/ And see if there is any wicked way in me,/ And lead me in the way everlasting."

2. QUESTION: I seem to have many of the symptoms of a victim of abuse but I have no memory of anything occurring. How do I know if I've repressed memories?

First and foremost, I always encourage people who believe they may have repressed something to begin with prayer. In my own life, I began praying Psalm 51:6 daily. Little by little God returned only those memories that I was ready to handle at the time.

Second, it is often helpful to find a credible counselor who is trained in this area to help you sort out your feelings and memories. The counselor should be knowledgeable about abuse issues, but in no way suggestive or intrusive. For instance, a counselor who would suggest after one visit that he is sure you were molested by your father, even though you have no memory of such, or that you suffered ritual abuse as a child, is a person to avoid. A good clinician walks a delicate balance similar to a skilled physician. A physician who has been in practice for several years acquires enough knowledge, after seeing symptoms repeatedly, to know what needs further exploration and testing. So it is with a good clinician. On the basis of all the information provided by the client, including the client's history, symptoms, and presenting problems, the clinician explores possibilities with the client without making snap decisions or in any way leading a client to certain conclusions.

This does not mean that, once the client has remembered or recounted certain incidents, the clinician may not use her expertise to help name and define what the client is describing. For instance, a client may be able to describe how each evening her father came home from work, drank a few beers, and then lined the children up and walloped them for some minor infraction. She may remember these events without ever having recognized that she grew up in an abusive, alcoholic home. The important factor here is that the client is providing the information. The clinician is merely helping to define it.

One primary principle I teach in my seminars and in the support groups I lead is a scriptural concept that is very appropriate here. Matthew 13:12 states: "For whoever has, to him more will be given, and he will have abundance; but whoever does not have, even what he has will be taken away from him." I have known many people who have been so concerned about what they *don't* know about their past that they have failed to deal with what they *do* know. In other words, if I have a client who suspects she may have repressed memories, we do not begin by searching for something we are not certain is there. Instead, I teach my clients this scriptural principle: *we must first appropriate the knowledge God has already given them before He will entrust them with more.* It is through what is known and processed that we often find the door to the unknown.

I find that God often protects clients from certain memories until they have gained enough skill to deal with what has been repressed. Some of these necessary tools are acquired through dealing with current family issues as well as identifying dysfunctional patterns from their families of origin. As they learn about processing their emotions, setting healthy boundaries, roles within the family, and better communication skills, they are better equipped to face anything that might surface from the past.

If you are a person who fears you may have repressed something, don't go on a quest for the memory, pulling out the family photo album and analyzing pictures of relatives to see who looks a little strange. Relax, pray and seek God for His wisdom, truth, and direction. Remember, it is the Holy Spirit's job to "lead us into all truth." I have found Deuteronomy 29:29 especially helpful regarding this issue. It says: "The secret things belong to the LORD our God, but those things which are revealed belong to us and to our children forever, that we may do all the words of this law."

3. QUESTION: How do I know if what I am remembering is accurate?

Unfortunately, there is no formula that can test repressed memories for accuracy. The best I can do is help by explaining how repressed memories often surface and what general characteristics they have. Generally, repressed memories come to consciousness in pieces or tidbits. They may be vivid or vague depending on where you are in the process of remembering. The most important thing to realize is that repressed memories are like puzzle pieces. They begin to fit together as you spend time sorting and framing the puzzle.

An example may help to illustrate. If I were to hand you a single puzzle piece from a 500-piece puzzle and ask you to tell me all about the puzzle, you would not be able to do so. But if you were to begin sorting the pieces by color or shape and piecing them together, the puzzle would soon begin to make more sense. That is why it is so vital to obtain the assistance of someone who can help you sort out the pieces and begin framing the puzzle of your past.

Repressed memories may come to the surface in several different ways. Some people experience flashbacks where they actually re-experience the memory after being triggered by some external stimuli. Others experience body memories in which their body remembers what happened before their conscious mind does. Those who report body memories often experience pain, stiffness, or even numbness in certain parts of the body. In a body memory, the body physically reenacts what it experienced during a violation, even though the person has no conscious recollection of the event. Still others begin to experience their repressed memories primarily through emotions and/or dreams. It is imperative that considerable time be taken to sort out what may be coming through these different avenues. I encourage clients to pray, diligently taking each new piece before God and asking Him to confirm and add to what appears to be vague and disconnected. God must be allowed to remove any images or pieces that are not based in truth. I always caution those in the process of remembering to keep this information between themselves and a counselor until the puzzle has taken shape and there is no doubt about the memories and the events that took place. Many victims make the mistake of confronting family members or their perpetrator in the early stage of remembering, which can be devastating for everyone.

The crucial part of victims' initial remembering is to trust themselves and God with what is being remembered. I have had numerous victims later discover many pieces of evidence corroborating what they initially remembered. There have been some cases where criminal convictions have been made on the basis of a repressed victim's testimony—some events having occurred over thirty years prior.

Recently there has been concern over what is termed *false memory recall*. Unfortunately, there are those who have invented memories or who have been susceptible to suggestive input. However, the number of those within this category is insignificant compared to the number of viable and verifiable incidents of abuse.

Finally, if you continue to be uncertain about incidents or flashes that are coming to mind, wait and pray. God will be faithful to lead you in the path of truth as you seek Him and employ the safeguards I have suggested in this and other questions.

4. QUESTION: Why would God want us to remember those events anyway?

Of course, I cannot fully answer what God's reasons are for having us remember certain events, but I can share a glimpse of what He has seemed to impress upon me regarding this question. I don't believe God brings these memories back just so we will remember all the horrible details of what we have experienced. He brings them back to us for our instruction, healing, and entrance into greater freedom. This is why it is so crucial to depend on God's timing and not our own in the process of remembering.

Many times the memories hold within a woundedness that has paralyzed us for years. Until God brings us the memory, we are held captive to emotions, behaviors, and faulty thinking.

The revealing of the memory is only the first step in a process that eventually leads to freedom.

Ginny, my dear friend, had struggled with being the classic codependent. She was always there to offer a helping hand to those in need. She found herself driven toward doing things for others and was consumed with guilt if she thought she had let someone down. Ginny had few of the dramatic symptoms of victimization: she'd never been promiscuous, never suicidal, had no chemical addictions, and had never experienced extreme depression. She only sought therapy after feeling prompted by the Lord to explore why it was that, at thirty-eight, she had a severe stomach ailment that could not be conclusively diagnosed. She also had no memory of her bedroom at the home in which she had lived from the ages of six through seventeen.

After months of therapy, her memories emerged. She had been sexually abused by her father from age four. Since she was an only child, there was no other sibling to confer with regarding the shocking memories that were surfacing. Ginny had a hard time believing what she was seeing in her mind and experiencing through body memories. Although she'd prayed for truth, she was convinced that what she was recalling could not be true because her father had always been her greatest supporter. Even now, her father was extremely involved in her life and the lives of her children. He was a doting father and generous grandfather.

Early in her therapy, there was no information on repression, and Ginny thought she must be crazy. Over time, however, God revealed more and more pieces that made the puzzle of her life fit together. An important part of Ginny's healing came when she could believe herself and God, and trust that what He was bringing to her was true. After months of struggling she no longer begged for evidence to confirm what she already knew.

Eight years after her initial memories, her cousin came forward with her own memory of abuse perpetrated by Ginny's father. Her cousin asked her one day, "Do you remember the fountain?" With that simple question, Ginny's mind flooded with the horror of additional memories that God later used to show her the root of her codependency.

Her father had taken both Ginny and her cousin to his workplace one Saturday. He took her cousin into the bathroom to the fountain (a wash basin) and molested her. Ginny, about six at the time, was left alone outside the bathroom door to hear the screams of her cousin begging her for help. Ginny knew what was going on in that bathroom. It had happened to her as well. The Lord revealed to her how on that day she had vowed never to leave someone in need again and that from then on, at all costs, she would rescue anyone who needed it. Ginny is convinced that God's purpose for revealing this memory was to help her understand how it had impacted her entire life and how Jesus wanted to set her free from the devastating hurt and betrayal that surrounded this event. She now realizes that in every memory God has brought to her, there has been a pearl of wisdom and a measure of greater healing.

I am firmly convinced that *God brings these memories to us in order to remove any obstacles that keep us from knowing the truth about ourselves and, more importantly, about Him.* Throughout Scripture He tells us of His character and His desire that we might know Him. I believe Satan continually tries to distort who God really is. When we experience hurtful events, the enemy is there sowing seeds of destruction and distortion. These seeds take the form of untruthful messages about ourselves and God that, when left unchecked, become our faulty assumptions and beliefs. As we seek God for His truth, He will expose the enemy's lies, uproot them, and plant the truth in our hearts.

Throughout Scripture God admonishes His people to look back to the many times He delivered them and was faithful to them. He also reminds them of their errors and how they forsook Him for foreign gods, turning aside from His provision and care. Although as victims of abuse we are not responsible for someone else's sin against us, we do bear the consequence of that sin and often respond to it in unhealthy, sinful, and destructive ways. God brings these events and our responses to them to our awareness in order to restore to us His love, provision, and protection. It was sin and its consequences that grieved God's heart to such an extent that He sent His own dear Son as the price for our victory over sin and its consequences.

5. QUESTION: I have several friends who have been in counseling for abuse and other issues from their childhood. I graduated from a Bible college and frankly, have been troubled by the concept of the *inner child* as talked about by my friends. This seems to be a New Age concept. Please clarify what you mean when you use the term *child within* [see chapter four].

First of all, let me clarify that I am not in complete agreement with how others may use this or similar terms in the psychological community. I, too, have been troubled by some of the mystical and questionable practices of many who espouse this term. I cannot guarantee that everyone uses it in the same way or with the same foundation as I. I *can* tell you what I have come to believe and found to be scripturally based.

Several years ago, after walking through considerable healing with the Lord and ministering to many across the country, I asked Him to show me an illustration that would help people to understand the concept of the inner child. A few weeks passed. Then, one morning while sitting at the breakfast table with my two daughters, I heard the Lord ask me, *Jan, what do you see?* At the time I was looking at my oldest daughter, Heather, who was seven. I said, *Lord, I see Heather, my daughter.*

Again He said to me, *Jan, what do you see?* I looked around the table more intently, knowing I was surely missing something and then replied, *Lord, I see Heather. She's seven years old. I see Kellie, who's five, and some cereal boxes and milk.* The third time the Lord said to me, *Jan, what* else *do you see?*

In that instant it was as though a veil lifted from my eyes, and while gazing at my daughter Heather, I no longer saw her at seven. I saw that special day—September 12, 1981—when I lay on the delivery table and the doctor picked up my little child and said, "It's a girl."

Another flash came. I saw the day Heather took her first tiny step unassisted when we were vacationing in Lake Tahoe. Next I flashed to that monumental day in September 1986, when Heather proudly marched off to kindergarten, lunch pail in hand and a huge smile on her face, while I wiped the tears from my eyes and acknowledged the reality that my little girl was growing up.

All of these scenes flashed before my eyes as I looked across the table at my Heather. The events were an integral part of my child, none of which I could separate. The Lord said to me, *Jan, so it is with* my *children. Not only do I see you in the present, but I see every event that has taken place in your life to bring you to the present.* He also sees the future and who we are becoming in Him.

I realized then, in greater dimension, the immenseness of our God. *He is not limited to time and space as you and I know it.* I believe that in my recovery He literally stepped back into time to administer healing to the child in me—a child who desperately needed a loving Father to bring comfort and healing. I have experienced this divine intervention many times over the last thirteen years and have had the privilege of witnessing God touch others in the same way. Psychology cannot do this. Even a good counselor cannot perform such a life changing experience. Only the God of all comfort, who is the same yesterday, today, and forever, can transcend time to heal the broken-hearted and set the captive free.

I saw in this whole experience a glimpse of God's eternal perspective. He who sits on the circle of the earth is not bound by the limitations of this earthly life. He calls us His children and beckons us to come to Him with all that wearies us and loads us down. Jesus said, "Let the little children come to Me, and do not forbid them; for of such is the kingdom of heaven" (Matt. 19:14).

Unfortunately, many who were hurt in childhood try to rid themselves of that wounded child's pain by forgetting it, shoving it aside, or burying it deep within. They often inadvertently rid themselves of a quality that is a requirement of the kingdom: their childlikeness. Jesus said, "Unless you change and become like little children, you will never enter the kingdom of heaven" (Matt. 18:3 NIV). It is because of this requirement that I believe God brings us to the point of reckoning with our past pain. He desires to bring life and restoration through the healing of wounds, so that we might enter into His kingdom as children.

Those of us who were abused as children lost some very precious qualities that God wants to revive: vulnerability, total dependence, trust, spontaneity, honesty, faith without fear, and expectant love. I have seen in my own life how, through the healing of hurts, God has redeemed to me the years the locusts had eaten. He brought resurrection life to the child within me. I often quote 2 Samuel 14:14, as it speaks to me of God's beckoning love: "But God does not take away life; instead he devises ways so that a banished person may not remain estranged from him" (NIV). God does plan ways to bring all those banished children to Himself, where at last they will be comforted, safe at home in the Father's arms.

6. QUESTION: I have heard you speak about the importance of grieving over the losses of our childhood, but I'm not sure how to do this. Why is this so necessary?

First of all, grieving is a scriptural concept. Throughout the Old Testament are many kings and prophets who, when faced with calamity, impending defeat, or recognition of sin, tore their garments and put on sackcloth and ashes—the outward symbol of mourning or grieving. Unfortunately in Western culture, we have lost the value and significance of grieving as portrayed in Scripture. When someone experiences loss, we allow him three days to attend the funeral and put back his happy face.

This was not so in the early Judaic culture. Elizabeth Kubler-Ross, while researching in her work with terminal patients, found that the Judaic culture understood grieving as a process that took time. They incorporated the following when faced with a death or significant loss: three days of deep grieving, seven days of mourning, thirty days of gradual adjustment, and eleven months of remembrance and healing. They recognized the need for an extended period of time to sufficiently grieve a loss.

We have become a society expecting instantaneous resolve. This mind-set has even crept into the church, causing many to err in their understanding of their walk with God and acceptance of their human frailties. We are told in Joel 2:12-13 (NIV):

> "Even now," declares the LORD,/ "return to me with all your heart,/ with fasting and weeping and mourning./ Rend your heart/ and not your garments./ Return to the LORD your God,/ for he is gracious and compassionate,/ slow to anger and abounding in love,/ and he relents from sending calamity."

The step of experiencing these feelings, described earlier in the book, is the crucial step of grieving, but one that many want to bypass. Most of us would rather talk about the pain than feel it. We find ourselves analyzing what happened and our responses to it rather than weeping and mourning and taking our broken hearts to the One who can mend them.

The losses associated with living in a fallen world are many. Specific losses related to sexual abuse include the loss of innocence, trust, safety, childhood, appropriate love from the offender, and protection, just to name a few. It is because of these many losses that the grieving process cannot be accomplished in only a few sessions or in a one-time prayer, no matter how sincere that prayer. In my personal experience, I found that it took about five years to walk through the process and grieve over the many losses that touched my life.

If you have never really gone through the tears and gut-wrenching sobs that seem to last forever, the questions and confusion, and the anger toward your offenders and even God, you probably have not allowed the Holy Spirit to reach into the depths of your pain. Even though grieving was excruciating, it was often in this place that God's love touched me and brought me the greatest comfort. I am now so glad that I did not short-circuit this step, but walked through the "valley of the shadow of death" knowing He would be with me.

Three scriptures have been of comfort and promise to me in this anguish-filled step:

- Psalm 126:5: "Those who sow in tears/ Shall reap in joy."
- Psalm 30:5: "Weeping may endure for a night,/ But joy comes in the morning."
- Psalm 84:6-7: "As they pass through the Valley of Baca [tears],/ They make it a spring;/ The rain also covers it

with pools./ They go from strength to strength;/ Each one appears before God in Zion."

7. QUESTION: I have been told I am dishonoring my parents by looking at some of the issues of my past. How can I honor my parents and go through recovery at the same time?

I believe it is possible to honor your parents and the position they were given by God without condoning or excusing what they did. I once heard Rich Buhler, a Christian radio talk show host, comment on this by saying, "It is similar to what we do with past presidents of the United States. We can honor the position this person has held without agreeing or supporting everything their administration stood for." To take this one step further, we can esteem the position and yet expose the inequities and failures of the one who has held such a position.

Charles Sell, in his book *Unfinished Business*, states, "Truth is the issue, not love or loyalty. Love covers a multitude of sins, but it should not distort them."[1]

One of the tragic mistakes made by Christians is failing to look at the dysfunctional patterns in their families of origin which may inadvertently be repeated with their own children. Once identified, these dysfunctional patterns can be dealt with and replaced by a healthier pattern, breaking the generational sin cycle. (My husband Don and I found this to be true in our early years in marriage and we discuss it in our book entitled *When Victims Marry*.)

It is possible to walk through recovery—being honest, truthful, and even angry about our experiences—and still maintain honor in our hearts toward our parents. I believe that Scripture gives us countless examples of those honored by both God and humankind whose lives were marked by horrendous failure and inconsistency. It might be helpful for you to read some of the account between David and King Saul in the Old

Testament. David continually modeled a reverence for the position God had given Saul while exposing Saul's motives and sin.

God never whitewashed the accounts of our patriarchs' lives. Rather, He brought all into the light to be seen—and forgiven. So it should be with us. We can choose to see our parents in reality, face what has been destructive, and follow the only One who can forgive and restore to us what has been lost.

8. QUESTION: Is confrontation always necessary? When would it not be appropriate?

A face-to-face confrontation with the perpetrator is not always necessary or even advisable. I do find, however, that some form of confrontation—through role-playing, letter writing, or journalizing—is helpful to the person going through recovery. In effect, it gives the adult part of us the opportunity to stand up and speak for the child part of us who could not do so. This is often very healing, whether or not the perpetrator ever knows it has occurred. I have had clients whose perpetrator was deceased go to the grave site and confront the person there. Others have worked through these issues in my office and do not feel the need to confront in person.

Confrontation is not advisable when there is a history of violence or mental illness which could put the survivor or other members of the family at risk. I do not advise confrontation in the case of satanic ritual abuse, as it most always results in more devastation to the victim. Confrontation is often not advisable if the perpetrator is a distant relative, family friend, or person with whom the victim has had little or no contact for years.

Confrontation of an offender is a personal matter which should be evaluated on an individual basis with the help of a professional or pastoral counselor. It should *only* be undertaken after seeking God and after a thorough examination of motives and readiness has been assessed. I have counseled many people over the years who stepped into confrontation that resulted in a further shattering of their lives. The importance of God's leading and timing in this issue cannot be emphasized enough. If God is not in it, the confrontation will not bear the fruit of healing nor offer the consolation that His heart desires for those who have suffered.

I have found that many people look to confrontation with unrealistic hopes and often rush into it prematurely. They have idealized a positive response which rarely happens. In effect, they are imagining that an unhealthy person or family will, with confrontation, see the error of their ways, acknowledge their responsibility, and embrace and love the survivor for providing this long-concealed information. Unfortunately, this is almost never the case when a family member or extended family is confronted with past abuse. In fact, it is often the opposite. The abuse survivor is ostracized, accused of blaming the family for their personal problems, spiritually rebuked for being unforgiving, or at best, ignored.

Because this reaction is more the norm, I work very carefully and closely with clients regarding confrontation. We examine their motivation, their expectations, and their goals, and thoroughly discuss the ramifications of such a confrontation within their particular family system. If, after these steps, it appears to be *in the best interest of the client* to confront, we will spend many sessions reviewing the content of what will be said, role-playing several different scenarios of response, and discussing how the relationship will be affected after confrontation has taken place.

What are some of the circumstances that might make confrontation necessary?* Many survivors find it necessary to confront when there are children in the family who may be at

---

*Minors should not confront their perpetrators unless it is done within a therapeutic environment with an adult advocate.

risk. This may be the case when an adult survivor knows that her perpetrator has access to minor children. In this case, the adult survivor would need to discuss with a professional the reporting laws in her state to determine whether or not a report should be made. Second, the survivor would have to decide who should be informed within the family and how this should take place. If the survivor has never confronted the perpetrator about her abuse, timely steps must be taken to insure both the safety of potential victims and herself.

Other survivors find confrontation necessary when the perpetrator is a close relative or friend of the family with whom they have frequent contact. They find it too difficult to maintain even a superficial relationship with the offender and have a need to address the past abuse openly. My own confrontation with my mother and stepfather came as a result of much prayer and a desire to have a relationship based on truth. I was prepared for denial and had determined that if my parents refused to "walk in the light and truth," I could not continue a relationship with them. This did not mean that I had not forgiven them. It only meant that if they did not acknowledge their need for forgiveness, I could not force them to accept mine. It is similar to the way God deals with unbelievers. Although Christ has truly paid the penalty for all sin, if an unbeliever chooses not to admit or confess his need for forgiveness there can be no harmony or unity.

Not all survivors who choose to confront have a desire to maintain a relationship with the offender. Confrontation is then a step for breaking the silence and severing the invisible hold the offender has had in her life. It is the reclaiming of a precious child of God who was exiled through no fault of her own.

Finally, it is important to note here that there is life after confrontation. Some who have successfully confronted soon realize that this step did not automatically put everything back together in their lives. Even though my stepfather acknow-ledged his responsibility, it was not the end of my recovery journey. There were many losses that had yet to be grieved, distortions that needed to be corrected, and wounds that needed to be healed. This took place over a season of time which I know was individually designed by the Master Potter, who reshapes and restores all broken vessels who surrender themselves to His loving hands.

9. QUESTION: I am a mother whose adult daughter just disclosed that she had been abused by my father. I'm feeling at a loss as to how best to respond to my daughter. What can I say or do to help?

First of all, it is of primary importance that you affirm your daughter by acknowledging that you believe her. You will need to ask your daughter how you can best support her in this process. You need to know that she will probably go through a period of anger toward you for not protecting her. This is sometimes very difficult for mothers who feel they were un-aware of what was happening. The mother often becomes defensive and places responsibility back on the child by saying things like, "If only you had told me, I would have protected you."

Whether or not you really knew about the abuse, children instinctively feel moms and dads are all-knowing protectors. One of the most healing responses you can give your daughter is that you are sorry for not seeing what was happening to her and for not taking appropriate steps to protect her. Even if you genuinely did not realize anything was occurring at the time, it is necessary for you as the parent to take the proper respon-sibility for protecting your child.

It is significant that research indicates eighty percent of

sexually abused children have mothers who were also abused in childhood. Although this does not always mean that the daughter is abused by the same person as the mother, in some cases it is the very same perpetrator. Whenever I counsel a mother, I encourage her to explore her own past to see whether or not there are abuse issues that have never been exposed or resolved. For some, it is difficult to understand the connection between a child who is abused and the percentage of mothers who were also abused. There are several factors that may contribute to this phenomena.

First, it has unfortunately been confirmed in research that mothers who were abused by certain family members in their childhood often allow their own children to have contact with the perpetrator. I believe this has to do with the misconception that the abuser would never molest anyone else. One reason for this is the mother's irrational belief that it happened to her only because she was bad or somehow deserved it. Children have a simplistic thinking: *Bad things happen to bad people. This bad thing happened to me. I must be bad*. Because the mothers have not appropriately seen the acts of abuse as connected solely with the perversion of the perpetrator, they will tend to believe it won't happen to their own or other children. Therefore, they do not prohibit contact.

Second, women who were abused as children and have not worked to resolve these issues through counseling often end up in one of two extreme conditions along a continuum. The first condition is what I call *hyper-vigilance*. This is characterized by the mother who, because of her own abuse, has become extremely cautious and fearful that something terrible will happen to her child. She scrutinizes and screens every action of the child and through her overly protective measures instills fear in the child. As a result, the child never learns her own proper assertive skills and can become a likely target for a perpetrator. The child will exhibit fearfulness and a learned helplessness from her mother that may set her up as a candidate for victimization.

The second condition is similar to what was described previously. It is the abused mother whose denial acts as blinders, preventing her from clearly seeing who is safe for her children and who is not. Because her denial is so strong, she often ignores warning signs or indicators of danger. She does not see certain behaviors as inappropriate or does not trust her intuition, discounting any feelings of discomfort that may arise from a given incident or person.

You may find in the course of your daughter's recovery that she may need some separation from you for a period of time. If you can respect her need for this without becoming defensive or manipulative through guilt, it will be most beneficial for the future relationship.

Know that your daughter may need to ask you some very difficult questions. She may need to talk about the issues more than once. In fact, she needs to be given time to work through her feelings and have the freedom to talk with you many times about what has gone on in the family and in your own life, and how the abuse made her feel. As a mother, this will be very painful and will evoke many emotions, including guilt, anger, and betrayal. It would be good for you to find your own counselor to help you deal with the issues and feelings that surface in your life as a result of this disclosure.

As I said before, the best message you can give your daughter is that she did not deserve what happened, that it was not her fault, and that you as her mother take a measure of the responsibility.

10. QUESTION: What about men who were abused as boys? Do they exhibit the same symptoms as women?

Unfortunately, men who were abused as boys often do not

even identify what happened to them as abuse. We have found in working with men some key differentials that should be noted.

First, men in our culture do not identify themselves as *victims* because it is not consistent with the macho image for a man to be a victim of anything. Researchers have found that to accurately assess the incidents of abuse with men the language must be changed. For instance, if I were addressing an audience of a hundred men and I asked the question, "How many of you were victims of sexual abuse as a boy?," maybe one in twenty-five would raise his hand. If, however, I asked those same men, "How many of you had *a sexual encounter of some type* as a boy?" about one in six would raise his hand.

In our culture, boys are treated very differently from girls when it comes to their sexuality. An illustration may be helpful. If a thirteen-year-old girl is having sex with a ninteen-year-old man, we define it by law as statutory rape and a punishable crime. If, however, a thirteen-year-old boy is having sex with a ninteen-year-old woman, we pat that boy on the back and say, "Heh, heh, he's sowing his wild oats."

Many men do not realize the negative impact of certain boyhood exploits or sexual encounters because they are generally encouraged to experiment with their sexuality far more than girls. I have met hundreds of men over the years who, although they had experienced abuse, never saw it as such. Nor did they connect the abuse with the resulting symptoms in their adult life. I'll never forget a teacher of mine who had an obvious problem with pornography and was extremely inappropriate in his behavior and conversation with females in the class. When discussing the whole area of sexual abuse, he held the position that abuse is only harmful to children if the conditions surrounding it are violent or intimidating to the child. He asserted that *friendly* abuse has no negative impact on a child. We debated this issue quite often, with me contending that *all* sexual encounters experienced by children result in damage to the child and subsequent difficulties in adult life. My teacher adamantly disagreed, stating that he had been abused in a friendly context and he was proof that there were no negative by-products! I appreciated his disclosure and rested my case. Later it was discovered that he had molested at least one child in his extended family.

We must remember that God created our sexuality as something good. It is sacred and is to be protected. When we have been abused, even within a friendly context, someone has violated a part of us that God intended to be set apart for one person and place—our mate within marriage.

Men who were abused as boys often find it difficult to come forward and admit they were overpowered or intimidated by another person. Boys who *let* this happen are seen as wimps or blamed for not stopping it. If a boy is molested by an older female, he experiences all kinds of confusion. He is encouraged by society at large to explore and initiate his sexual prowess with females, but as a child he feels shame and guilt over what is happening. Unable to deal with this confusion, many men normalize or repress these events in an effort to convince themselves that there was no harm done.

Men who were abused may exhibit many of the characteristics noted in previous pages. However, I have found men to have some distinctive symptoms that may set them apart from women who have experienced abuse. First, men may develop homophobia (especially if they were abused by a male perpetrator). Homophobia is a fear of homosexuality. Men who were abused by males may develop a fear of becoming homosexual or fear that the experience itself may be indicative of homosexuality. Some men who feel this way may exhibit an extreme hostility or anger toward homosexuals, while others may counter their fear by becoming sexual conquerors of women to prove their virility and masculinity.

It is not, however, widely recognized that many men and women who have ended up in the homosexual lifestyle were abused as children, primarily because those within the prohomosexual community do not wish to expose the link between their abuse and their lifestyle. If there was such a connection, homosexuality could be linked to environmental causes rather than *inborn predisposition*, as the activists promote. In my ten years of counseling, I have found that as high as eighty percent of the homosexuals I have encountered were abused in childhood. I am not asserting abuse as the cause, but I have found it to be a major contributor in the lives of those who become homosexual.

Second, a common distinctive symptom in men is the development of sexual addiction. A sexual addiction, depending on the stage, may take the form of an obsessive need for sex within the marriage, an addiction to pornography or X-rated movies, masturbation, illicit sexual affairs, and frequenting of adult book stores, massage parlors, or topless bars. Women who were abused may also develop sexual addictions, but it is far more common in men. Unfortunately, men who are in the early stages of sexual addiction may not identify it as a problem, and it only escalates if not addressed.

I've found that many men who were abused as boys were exposed to pornographic material as a part of the abuse. The exposure to this material creates an appetite that is unhealthy and fosters information about sex and sexuality that is destructive. Unfortunately, we have been desensitized through the media as to how harmful this material is. Even within the church, many have compromised their values as what is portrayed by the media becomes increasingly explicit. We have bought the lie that says *whatever we do in the privacy of our own home is okay* or *viewing this will only enhance our sexual relationship*.

The sexual relationship is a wonderful gift from God, but not the sole means of obtaining intimacy within the marriage relationship. Unfortunately, men who have a sexual addiction look to the sexual aspect of the relationship to meet all their intimacy needs. One of the primary messages of pornography is that women are objects to be used for sexual gratification, not persons to be valued. Both men and women who have been abused must learn how to develop a trusting and intimate relationship that is balanced in the physical, emotional, and spiritual realms in order to experience the fulfillment God intended for marriage.

Third, men who have been abused may have an erratic job history. Due to the abuse, they often report personality conflicts at work that result in termination or relocation. Their difficulty with authority figures may be linked to their anger toward their perpetrator, who was more powerful and controlling than they. If these issues are not resolved, they may show up in the workplace as well as at home.

Fourth, men who experience abuse as boys may shut off their emotions. They are disconnected from themselves and their feelings. They cannot cry or empathize with others because they have numbed themselves to their own painful past. Women who are married to these men often describe them as *robotic* in their approach to life. There is little joy, enthusiasm, or zest—they live life on the flatlands and avoid the peaks and valleys of emotion.

Finally, men who were abused by a female perpetrator may exhibit all of the previous symptoms, and also develop a hatred of women, just as some female abuse victims develop a hatred of men. This hatred may manifest itself in a myriad ways. They may have difficulty developing healthy sexual intimacy within the marriage, or they may become withdrawn, or they may become controlling. These men must come to recognize that past abuse was detrimental to their overall development. Like women who were abused, they must work through the painful process of grieving the losses and allow God's healing presence to restore the child within them who is so precious to God.

11. QUESTION: Is the recovery process for men the same as for women?

Much of the process of healing is the same for men and women. They must (1) Face the problem, exploring the symptoms and by-products of the abuse in their adult life; (2) Recount the incident(s) with a counselor, support group, or knowledgeable support person; and (3) Experience the feelings of loss and grief from the child's perspective. For many men, these steps will seem foreign and needless. They often want to *think* the process rather than *feel* the process.

When speaking to groups across the country about the recovery process, I spend a great deal of time on step three, as it is so vital to overcoming an abusive past. When we are vulnerable enough to grieve from the depths of our being before our God and another human being, we allow ourselves to receive consolation and comfort from the One who has truly borne our griefs and sorrows.

For both men and women who have been abused, there is a tendency to want to bypass this pain. If you do, you will be robbing yourself of knowing Christ in both the power of the resurrection and the sharing in the fellowship of His sufferings (Phil. 3:10).

For men who were abused, it is especially important to find other men with whom they can develop a close, healthy relationship. A significant finding among boys who are abused is that many of them had fathers who were physically or emotionally absent during their growing up years. This leaves a young boy to define his own masculinity and sense of manhood. Unfortunately, there are those who prey upon boys in this vulnerable state, devastating them through abuse and sentencing them to a life with little ability to connect with others in a meaningful way. Having other men they trust can help repair the damage through a genuine, mutual relationship.

12. QUESTION: Is professional counseling always necessary? Isn't it possible for God to heal without obtaining outside help?

God is certainly able to heal us without any outside help. However, I have found that He often does not choose to do so. This does not mean that those who do not seek professional help will not be healed. God will accomplish His good pleasure with all who are committed to Him.

I have found, though, that healing is expedited through the counseling process, for several reasons. First, counseling on a regular basis helps us to be accountable. Too many of us, myself included, find it difficult to maintain a consistent pattern of working through painful issues unassisted. It is far too easy to avoid, deny, or ignore the pain without someone to encourage and support us in the process.

Second, the insight and objectivity of others is essential in viewing circumstances and events that we have unknowingly either distorted or "normalized" through our own subjectivity. One of the foundational issues for men and women in need of healing is the ability to trust. For most of us this is not instantaneous but a process that occurs over time, in several spheres of our lives, through various relationships. Looking back over my own healing, I see that God used many different relationships—those with my children, with a therapist, with other support group members, those between my husband and my daughters, and my relationship with Him—to accomplish His work.

I've discovered a key principle: *When we've been sinned against relationally, God uses relationships to heal us.* He made us relational beings, just as He is, and when we have been hurt in the context of relationships, He desires to use healing relationships to accomplish restoration. This is His intention for the body of Christ. We are to walk alongside one another, comforting and ministering to each other as did the good Samaritan. It is interesting to note that Jesus emphasized a relational quality that makes Christians distinctive: "By this all will know that you are My disciples, *if you have love for one another*" (John 13:35, emphasis mine). He did not emphasize performance, intellectual understanding, or even doctrine—He emphasized love between the brethren.

I firmly believe that if we, as the body of Christ, were functioning as Christ intended, there would be no need for Christian counseling. Unfortunately, there are far too many believers whose own woundedness creates a hindrance in being able to effectively and compassionately assist others within the body. There are many well-meaning men and women who live life primarily in the cognitive or intellectual sphere. They have, for the most part, shut out the healing power of God from their own emotional sphere, and as a result have difficulty showing compassion or relating to those who are dealing with emotional pain. It is no coincidence that those who are often the most adamantly opposed to Christian counseling have grown up in dysfunctional, abusive homes and have "overcome" these hurts by walking in the opposite direction, avoiding their pain. Due to this, those who go to them for comfort find counsel similar to that which Job received—a message of condemnation rather than consolation.

This is contrary to all that we observe in the life of Jesus. He walked in the direction of pain. Hebrews 12:2 says we are to fix our eyes on Jesus, "who for the joy that was set before Him endured the cross, despising the shame." Likewise, Luke 9:51 says that "He steadfastly set His face to go to Jerusalem." It is not by walking away from, or around, our pain that we become victorious. It is by walking *through* the "valley of the shadow of death" with One who has journeyed the path before us.

Christian counseling does not heal us. Only God can heal us. But it is often through good, biblically based Christian counseling that we are positioned to receive the healing God wants to give. It is like going to an orthopedic surgeon when we have had a severe limb breakage: the doctor, with all his training and expertise, may place pins, reposition bones, and surgically repair surface tissue, but the healing depends on God and the wonderful mechanism He instilled in our bodies to accomplish such healing.

If you are wondering whether or not you need to obtain some assistance, commit a season of time to prayer, seek wise counsel from other mature, balanced believers, and wait for God to lead you in the direction of those who can assist you in the journey toward healing.

13. QUESTION: I have three children and am wondering what, if anything, I should tell them about my own abuse. How did you handle this with your two daughters?

I have been very truthful with my own daughters from the time they were very young. Early in recovery, when they would observe me crying and ask what was the matter, I would sit down with them and share that Mommie was hurt when she was a little girl and that some of her tears were about trying to get over that hurt. Other times, when I was angry or irritable, I would have to go to them and apologize, explaining that my anger was not their fault, but that Mommie was going to counseling to help get over the hurts that often made her angry. I would explain that they were not responsible for making me angry.

It is important to answer children in an honest, age-appropriate way. I had prayed from very early on that God would make clear to me when and if I was to tell my girls about my own abuse. I had been very general for several years, which seemed to satisfy their questions. The turning point came when Heather reached age seven.

Heather's second-grade teacher had asked me to come to Heather's class in the fall to share about being an author. I agreed and thought nothing of it. The girls had often heard me talking to people and in fact, would often go with me to the Christian book store and make it a game to try and find Mommie's book on the shelf. About a week before I was to speak in Heather's class, Heather looked at me seriously and said, "Mommie, I know you wrote *Door of Hope*, but just exactly what is *Door of Hope* about?" I breathed a quick prayer for wisdom and responded, "Well, Heather, you know how Mommie has always told you about being hurt when I was a little girl?"

"Yes, Mommie" she said.

"Well, *Door of Hope* is about how Jesus helped Mommie get over those hurts."

"How were you hurt, Mommie?" she asked curiously.

"You know, Heather, how Mommie has talked to you about good touching and bad touching?"

"Yes."

"When Mommie was a little girl, someone touched me in a bad way and that left Mommie with a lot of hurt inside."

"Who was it, Mommie?" she asked innocently.

In that instant, I knew the day had come. I took a deep breath and replied, "Heather, it was your Grandpa————." That year we were spending Thanksgiving with my parents, which was about a month away. I knew I needed to share further.

"Heather, Grandpa knows that what he did was very wrong. He and I have talked all about this and have worked things out between us. Your daddy knows what happened and Grandma also knows. We are planning to spend Thanksgiving at Grandma's house, but if knowing this information makes you feel the least bit uncomfortable around Grandpa, we will not go."

She thought for a minute and said, "No, Mommie, it's okay."

I then said, "Heather, it's okay for you to still care about Grandpa, even though what he did was very wrong. But, if you ever feel uncomfortable around him, I want you to come and talk to me about it, okay?"

"Yes, Mommie" she agreed.

Then wanting to affirm Heather, I said, "Heather, you're a bigger girl than Kellie now, and Kellie is a little too young to know about this, so I don't want you to tell her. When she gets to be a bigger girl like you, Mommie will tell her too. Okay?"

"Yes, Mommie," she said with a smile on her face.

Two days later, we were in the car discussing my plans to speak in Heather's classroom. Heather was on my right in the passenger seat, and Kellie was in the back seat. Out of Kellie's five-year-old mouth came the fated question, "Mommie, I know you're going to Heather's class. What is *Door of Hope* about?"

Heather looked over at me, rolling her big hazel eyes as if to say, "What are you going to do with this one, Mom?"

I prayed again, and very tentatively said, "Well, Kellie, you know how Mommie has told you that I was hurt when I was a little girl? *Door of Hope* is about how Jesus helped Mommie heal from that hurt."

Inquisitively she responded, "Where did this happen, Mommie?"

"In my home, honey" I said briefly, to which she immediately inquired, "Well, where was your momma?"

At that moment God showed me a powerful insight. Out

of the mouth of a little child came a significant realization. *Children expect their homes to be safe places and naturally assume that mommies protect them and make sure nothing bad happens to them.* Kellie had no idea of the impact that innocent question had on me. How powerfully it demonstrated the essence of betrayal a child feels when abused by a loved one or when unprotected by the primary source of protection God provides — a mother and father.

I was jolted back into the present as I saw Heather looking at me intently. I knew in that instant that it was not the time to disclose anything to Kellie. Looking out my window in an effort to distract my five year old and observing a plane overhead, I said, "What is that out there?" Kellie looked out her window, her focus shifting, and I recorded her previous question in my heart. Heather looked over at me and sighed with relief, as if to say, "You made it through that one, Mom."

I felt at the time that Kellie was too young to process that information, so I waited. I also must confess that I was concerned that my little Kellie, if given that information, might in her five-year-old curiosity march up to my dad during Thanksgiving dinner and ask, "Why did you hurt my mommie when she was a little girl?" I wasn't quite ready for that one over dinner!

When Kellie turned eight, God again orchestrated a situation in which Kellie began asking questions and at that time I sat down with her and disclosed in brief what had happened to me and by whom it had happened. Since then, I have asked my daughters how they felt about me sharing with them. Both said unequivocally that they were glad I had told them.

It is not necessary nor advisable to go into graphic detail with your children. As they mature there may be times when they will ask more specific questions and you will have to discern how much and to what extent you share. I do believe children should be told something for the sake of their own protection and education. It is especially pertinent information if your abuser is someone they have contact with or if they are married with children and their children may be protected through their awareness of past abuse.

If you do share your abuse with your children, you need to give them room to deal with it in their own way. My friend Ginny really struggled about telling her three children. She had a son in his mid-teens, a daughter in early adolescence, and a son in elementary school. She had pulled back in her relationship with her father, telling him he could no longer drop by or contact them unannounced. She did this without disclosing anything to her children and her father's absence resulted in the children questioning why Grandpa wasn't around anymore. To make matters more difficult, her father was sending the children notes, saying how much he missed seeing them, and her teenage son was inviting Grandpa over without her knowledge. She became the bad guy when it became obvious that she did not want Grandpa around. She had a terrible time deciding what to do, since her older son had been especially close to his grandfather, but she finally decided he must be told.

When her husband told their son about the abuse one afternoon, he left the house in rage. He felt he also had been betrayed by his grandfather. He was so angry he punched his fist through a fence and bloodied his hand. Eventually, though, his anger subsided and he again had a relationship with his grandfather, even though his mother maintained her need for separation.

In disclosing abuse to children, it is of utmost importance that you let them deal with their own emotions regarding the disclosure. You should not expect them to feel the same intensity that you do. Nor should you try to downplay their legitimate feelings of betrayal. It may be necessary for you to contact a counselor who can help them work through their feelings apart from you.

Finally, do not let others convince you that forgiveness means you never bring these issues up again or that it is safe to leave your children with this person now that things are out in the open. Even though I have truly forgiven my parents, I am still responsible before God to be wise and prudent regarding my own children. Thirteen years have passed since I confronted my parents. To this day, my children have never stayed at my parents' home, and I am always present when my dad is around my daughters. I told my parents when I confronted them years ago that this would be my policy concerning my children since they were unwilling to obtain help. Even if they obtained professional help I would choose to maintain this policy. I knew then, as now, that I did not want my girls to come to me in twenty years and say, "Mom, knowing what you knew, why did you let us stay with Grandpa?" I've counseled far too many young women who, even as adults, ask the same poignant question Kellie asked years ago, "Where was *my* Momma when all this was happening to me?"

14. QUESTION: I was abused by my father, who is now deceased. I have been in counseling, but have never told my aging mother about the abuse because I don't want to hurt her. Is it necessary to tell my mother?

This is a very difficult question to answer since I do not know the individual circumstances of your background or of the abuse. I can provide some factors for your consideration, but I would advise you to seek some professional help in order to better determine what course of action is the best for you.

First of all, it will be important for your own well-being to determine whether or not *you* have a need to tell your mother about the abuse. It sounds from your question that you have taken on a protective role which may actually inhibit your own process of recovery. It would be helpful for you to examine with a counselor your hesitancy in discussing these issues with your mother to determine whether or not your motives for silence are healthy.

Second, if your father abused you he was, in effect, unfaithful to your mother and broke their marriage covenant. If she genuinely was not aware of this, she may have a right to this information. However, you should be prepared for a less than favorable response.

Third, I have found that many women who were abused by their fathers have a very stormy relationship with their mothers, which seems unfounded. Many times they have felt alienated, distant, and unloved by their mothers, but have never been able to figure out why. Sometimes mothers in these situations see signs of inappropriate behavior from their husbands, fail to check out those signs, and blame their daughters for their husband's partiality. I have had several women say it was as if their mothers were jealous of them. How many of these women longed for their mothers to protect them from their fathers and yet were faced with accusations and undeserved anger!

Finally, I encourage you to pray for direction concerning this matter. One faulty assumption that many survivors make is that if they disclose this information, their elderly mother could be shocked into a stroke or death. It is important that *you* not take on the responsibility for your father's actions or the impact that information might have on your surviving parent. If your desire is to shed light on issues that have been hidden in darkness, in order that the remaining relationship can be based upon truth, God will honor your heart. The results must be left in His hands.

15. QUESTION: I'm finding that, as I work through the abuse from my childhood, I'm more angry with my mother than my father, who was my abuser. Is this normal?

Yes. I have found it to be very common in abusive and alcoholic homes for adult children to be angrier at the *enabling* parent than the abuser or alcoholic. This was certainly true in my own case, although I did not recognize it for several years. When I was in college, I used to write papers about my mother, identifying her as the person I most admired. For years I placed her on a pedestal for having the courage to put up with my stepdad's domineering and hostile demeanor. It was in my second go-around in counseling that God showed me the tremendous rage I had felt as a child for my mother's lack of protection. The child in me could not understand why my mother did not take definitive steps to ensure my safety. To me it was as if my mother continually chose my stepfather and his needs over mine. This pattern continued even into my adulthood, leaving me with a deep-rooted sense of unworthiness that plagued me for many years.

I also struggled through deep issues of rejection that took me several months of counseling to work through. I sensed even as a young child that I was unwanted, due to the turmoil of my parents' marriage. It was in those early years that I experienced what is known as *developmental injury* resulting from a lack of proper nurturing and bonding, primarily with my mother. For many who have been sexually abused, it is not only the abuse, but the context in which the abuse is placed, that is significant. My early development and the losses I experienced were as important as the abuse in forming my personality and coping styles.

My parents' divorce at age five left me feeling abandoned. Recently, the Lord showed me I had also harbored deep resentment toward my mother for "sending my Daddy away." I had vowed never to forgive her. Over the years I have repeatedly gone to the Lord with these and other deep hurts, acknowledging my own sinful response, and seeking His sufficient love to fill the void in my inner child's heart. God has reassured me through His Word that I am His precious child. Psalm 27:10 says: "When my father and my mother forsake me,/ Then the LORD will take care of me."

Several years ago in counseling, I was grieving the loss of my mother's love, feeling that if I did not have her love, I could not exist. In the midst of crying out to God from my broken heart, He led me to a verse that has been my comfort.

> . . . you whom I have upheld since you were conceived,/ and have carried since your birth./ Even to your old age and gray hairs/ I am he, I am he who will sustain you./ I have made you and I will carry you;/ I will sustain you and I will rescue you. (Isa. 46:3-4 NIV)

God gave us parents as models of His love for us. But all of us fail to perfectly exemplify His heart of love. Through the years I have learned that ultimately, every human relationship will fail us and that our deepest fulfillment comes as we surrender, forgive, and rest in the sufficiency of God's unchanging love.

16. QUESTION: I told my family about being abused by an older brother. At first, some family members were sympathetic, but now most of them are denying that anything like this ever occurred. I'm being ostracized. What can I do to convince them that I am telling the truth?

Unfortunately in this case, there is really nothing you can or need to do. It is very difficult for us when we have spoken the truth and are maligned, ostracized, and misrepresented. Many men and women have shared a similar scenario with me over the years and it is becoming more and more prevalent.

If in your family there is a situation where children are in danger, you may need to consult with a professional about any further action you need to take to insure the protection of potential victims. But you cannot make it your job to convince your family of the truth. You have offered them truth, which they have rejected. So many who have found themselves in this position spend hours, days, and months formulating letters, sending books and articles, and having endless conversations—often in their heads—about the *right* way to enlighten family members. This rarely results in any change and only revictimizes the survivor through the family's repeated disbelief and rejection. Ultimately you must release the situation to the only One who changes hearts and lives. It may require that you obtain some help in this process.

As Christians, we have been under a faulty assumption: *we cannot be in disharmony with our family and still be right with God*. Because of this assumption, many Christians make it their quest to ensure family harmony and thereby perpetuate the sin through lack of disclosure and denial. This is an unhealthy practice. I have found that many times, even though we have lost our families over these issues, God restores to us others within the body of Christ. However, this does not always take away the pain at the loss of our family. I have been encouraged by Mark 10:29-30 and Matthew 10:35-38:

> So Jesus answered and said, "Assuredly, I say to you, there is no one who has left house or brothers or sisters or father or mother or wife or children or lands, for My sake and the gospel's, who shall not receive a hundred-fold now in this time—houses and brothers and sisters and mothers and children and lands, with persecutions—and in the age to come, eternal life.

> For I have come to 'set a man against his father, a daughter against her mother, and a daughter-in-law against her mother-in-law'; and

'a man's enemies will be those of his own household.' He who loves father of mother more than Me is not worthy of Me. And he who loves son or daughter more than Me is not worthy of Me."

I knew thirteen years ago when the Holy Spirit was urging me to journey this path toward wholeness that it would probably result in discord and division within my family, and in fact, it has. However, I also know that the same God who prompted the journey promises to make all things work together for good.

Remember, there will come a day when *all* will come to the knowledge of the truth. Until then, try to be comforted by these words from Matthew 10:26: "Therefore do not fear them. For there is nothing covered that will not be revealed, and hidden that will not be known."

17. QUESTION: My seven-year-old daughter was sexually abused by my sixteen-year-old nephew two years ago. We immediately sought counseling for her and went through the legal requirements regarding reporting. Our child's counselor has said she has responded well and we've discontinued treatment. Is there anything else we should do for our daughter?

First of all, let me commend you for believing your child and obtaining professional help for her. It will be important for you to ask your daughter's therapist the above question, since she is more acquainted with the individual circumstances of your family. However, it is very vital for you to know that, even though you have obtained counseling for your daughter and she has seemed to respond well, it does not mean this issue is forever closed. It is essential for you as a parent to continue to monitor your child and be aware of signs that may indicate further help is needed.

I have found that the issues surrounding abuse are very

much developmental in nature. What I could deal with at twenty-seven was different from what I dealt with at thirty-five, and what I will deal with at fifty may be different from what I am dealing with at forty.

For children, it is especially helpful to reopen these issues at different points in their development: preadolescence, adolescence, or any time when the child is displaying intense emotions or has difficulties in relationships that may warrant intervention. Certain issues have to be reopened because we are not equipped to deal with them at an earlier point, or because our life circumstances change, producing a need for deeper levels of examination in issues we had touched on previously.

When I conduct seminars, I share with the audience that after *Door of Hope* was written, I felt led to go to graduate school to obtain a Master's degree in Marriage, Family and Child Counseling. As a part of my training, I was required to obtain a minimum of ten hours of individual counseling. I thought, *No problem*, since I'd been in therapy before. I began praying about whom to see professionally and was led to a Christian female psychologist who had been one of my instructors.

At the time, I was conducting nationwide seminars on the issue of sexual abuse and was convinced I had no real need to seek additional help. I'll never forget our third session together. We were going over some psychological tests I had taken and I said to my new therapist, "Well, what do you think I need—a couple, three months of therapy?"

She looked at me straightforwardly and said, "On the basis of what I see, you could leave *early* at six months or stay two years and have God do the work He wants to do in your life."

I'd love to tell you that I said to her, "Oh, thank you, wise counselor that God gave me." Instead, I looked her right in the eye and said, "You don't understand—I'm famous. I've written the book on this subject!"

She kindly said, "Well Jan, it's up to you."

I left that counseling session in utter depression. I was ready to call my publisher and say, "Take the book off the shelf—I'm not healed." But when I arrived home and began praying, the Spirit of God spoke tenderly to my heart, *Jan, I've healed you, but I want to do more. Are you willing?* I said, *Yes, Lord. I want all that You have for me.*

And so, I spent every week for two years in that counseling office and told the Lord in the midst of it that I would be there five years if He wanted me there. He did such a deep work within me that I would not trade for anything in the world. I've continued to ask the Lord to let no stone go unturned in my life, and I am open to receiving more counseling as He would direct.

Sometimes when I share this, victims or mothers of abused children become discouraged because they think this means it is never over. The truth is that we can be healed and set free from the bondage of our past, but we are also in the process of continual healing and will not arrive at the end until we see Jesus face to face. The Bible teaches us that we are being conformed to the image of His Son (Romans 8:29). This is a process that occurs over a lifetime. So it is with healing. As we grow and change, God ministers truth to us at each level of our development. As we progress, more truth and healing come which results in greater intimacy with God.

With your daughter, you will have to continue praying and asking God for discernment regarding her needs for continued help. It is often beneficial during the teenage years to provide a group experience for youths. Adolescence is a difficult time for them and giving them support and encouragement will hopefully help them as they deal with peers and eventual dating relationships.

Above all, pray. I've often shared with other mothers that, although I have educated my two daughters extensively, there are no guarantees. I have learned to release my girls to God, knowing that the same One who redeemed what appeared to be unredeemable in my life will also do so in theirs. I have claimed Isaiah 54:13 over my children. May it be a blessed promise for you as well: "All your children shall be taught by the LORD,/ And great shall be the peace of your children."

18. QUESTION: My wife was sexually abused as a child and has been in counseling for four months. I want to be supportive but it seems like things are getting worse. What can I do to be of help?

First of all, let me encourage you by saying you are not alone. Many spouses of victims echo your same frustrations. It is hard to understand why, after treatment has begun, things seem to get worse.

For a victim of abuse, the incidents of her past are similar to a festering wound that has been covered up for years. When the wound is exposed, it requires a cleansing that is often very painful. My husband, Don, shares a personal story about the early stages of my recovery, when we were vacationing in Lake Tahoe, California. He had saved for months in preparation for our family vacation in this lovely resort area. I had been in counseling about three months at the time. The first night in our condominium, after a nice dinner, we retired for the evening. Don leaned across the bed to hug and kiss me and I said emphatically, "Don't touch me, don't kiss me, you repulse me!" My husband shares that it crossed his mind to get the keys to the car and leave. He thought that if *this* is what he was in for, he wanted out now. By God's grace, he did not follow those initial instincts, but continued to love me even during the most difficult stage of my recovery.

It is during this stage that many who are reliving the violations of their past project some of the blame and anger

216

onto those closest to them. It is a season of the recovery that will not last forever, but one that can best be weathered by obtaining support through counseling.

It will be helpful during this time to ask your wife specifically what she needs from you. Most victims of abuse need someone to listen, validate, and comfort them in their pain. Sometimes this is especially difficult for men who are used to problem-solving. Many men make the mistake of wanting to *fix* the situation by confronting the offender, or by simply saying to their wives, "Why can't you get over this? It happened so many years ago, just forget it and move on!" Unfortunately, many women have earnestly tried to do this, but are unable because the pain that has been buried deep within them resurrects itself daily in their lives. It isn't until they can openly dig up that pain, examine it, and fully express it that they can eventually extricate themselves from it.

Supporting your wife will take the form of listening to her pain, holding her while she cries, giving her space to work on these issues without demanding a specific timetable for completion, and giving her a choice when it comes to the area of sexual intimacy. I have often shared with husbands that the degree to which they can be supportive without being demanding directly correlates to how expeditiously their wives make it through recovery.

You might find it helpful to read the book my husband and I wrote, *When Victims Marry*, since we address many of these issues in more detail. Also, Don has a cassette tape entitled *Are You a Victim of Your Wife's Past?* that many men and women have found helpful. This is available through our ministry office.

Don and I are soon to celebrate our fifteenth wedding anniversary. There were times when we both wondered if we would make it through the frustration, anguish, disappointment, and grief. But God used the pit of pain to develop within our relationship a wealth of intimacy that we now treasure and delight in. He has restored to us *every* area that before had suffered loss and devastation. I'm convinced that as you seek Him and prayerfully consider how you might be the husband God has called you to be, God will be faithful to complete the work He has begun in both you and your wife.

19. QUESTION: We are leading a support group through our church and have encountered a few women who were ritualistically abused as children. Do you believe the reports of this type of abuse and how can we best help those with this background?

There is no question that ritualistic abuse is a form of abuse all too common. Even though many are skeptical because of the lack of sufficient tangible evidence, I do believe that these horrific events happen to children. In the ten years I have counseled victims of abuse, I have met many who were victims of ritualistic abuse, some of which was related to the occult. I have not specialized in the area of counseling ritual abuse victims and have referred them to other professionals I have come to trust and who deal specifically with such abuse.

Because of the intensity and complexity of this type of abuse, I encourage victims to make sure they are with a trained Christian professional who has dealt with this form of abuse extensively. Unfortunately, many in the church who do not understand the psychological/emotional damage from this abuse treat it as a spiritual problem only, needing deliverance or exorcism. This approach is far too simplistic and can be harmful to a person who has suffered such abuse.

When leading a support group for victims of abuse, it is important to have a professional in an advisory capacity to help determine each potential member's group readiness and to help you recognize the extent of your limitations. In the ten years that I conducted support/therapy groups, I was very cautious regarding the participation of those who came from ritualistic abuse backgrounds, primarily because the group experience can trigger so much that it is often difficult for them to manage. As a professional, I was always in close contact with their individual therapist, assessing from week to week whether the group experience was beneficial and safe for them as well as the other group members. Many who specialize in helping ritual abuse victims find it helpful to have a homogeneous group of only those who have experienced ritual abuse, rather than a combination of nonritual abuse and ritual abuse survivors.

In terms of how you can best help: be sure you are realistic about your own limitations, be able to set good boundaries, and do not try to be the sole source of support for someone who comes from this type of background. Acquaint yourself with Christian professionals in your area who have worked with ritual abuse victims and be prompt at making referrals.

Finally, you can help by committing yourself to intercessory prayer on their behalf, providing occasional child care while they attend their counseling sessions, and consistently demonstrating the love of God by listening, comforting, and allowing them all the time they need to work through these difficult, but resolvable, issues.

20. QUESTION: Since I began working on my abuse issues I've had trouble in my relationship with God. It is difficult for me to pray, read my Bible, and attend church. I really love the Lord, but find such emptiness in pursuing anything spiritual. Am I doing something wrong?

My heart goes out to you as I remember so well those times in my own healing journey. It often seemed that God was no where to be found and that the Word of God no longer nourished me as it once had. Do not despair. This too shall pass!

I have discovered in my own walk with God that there are times we go through our own wilderness experience even as many of God's choicest vessels in Scripture did. I am convinced that it is during these times our hearts are opened up and we are faced with ourselves. It has been through these dark times that many of the distortions and faulty beliefs I have unknowingly held about God and myself have been exposed to the light of His truth. I am not sure exactly why or how this happens, but I see it throughout the Scripture—in Job's life, in David's psalms, and in the life of King Hezekiah: "God withdrew from him [Hezekiah], in order to test him, that He might know all that was in his heart" (2 Chron. 32:31). I really believe that God already knows what is in our hearts, even when we do not. He allows these barren times to help us grapple with our motives and our deepest desires and to examine where our treasures really lie.

Many victims of abuse who go through this lack of zeal feel extremely guilty and fear impending punishment from God. I believe God actually ordains many of these times in our lives to help us gain perspective and realize there is *nothing* we can do to gain more of God's favor or love than what Christ already did on the cross. He wants to free us from the performance mentality and legalism that has ensnared so many of His children.

Do not misunderstand me. I believe in feeding on the Word of God, attending church regularly, and having consistent fellowship and communion with God in prayer. But I also know that when we reach those difficult stages in our lives where we cannot seem to muster enough self-discipline or where we lack motivation in our pursuit of God, He sees our hearts and He does not condemn us. I always encourage my clients to continue to keep their communication open with God during these times, even if that communication sounds like, *Lord, I know Your Word says You will never leave me. But Father, right now You seem so distant, so unattainable. I'm not even sure if I really believe You are there for me.* I know God hears these prayers and His Word confirms that He will not turn away from those who have a broken and contrite heart (Psalm 51:17).

I do add one caution: when being honest with God about how you feel, remember that He is God. He tells us in Hosea 7 that those who speak lies against Him open themselves up to destruction. When we accredit to God something that is evil, Satan is often right there to reinforce the lie and malign God's character. We must carefully balance our sharing with God, without accusing Him or imagining evil against Him, because the enemy will use those thoughts and feelings as a wedge between us. Satan desires to cut us off from the very Source of our hope and healing.

I find during these times in my life that comfort and intimacy with the Lord is strengthened through music. I make it a point to listen to praise songs and to worship Him, even though I feel such contradiction between my life and the words on my lips. This, along with journaling to God, is my lifeline. Know that you are His precious child. He promises to be faithful even when we are faithless. Zephaniah 3:17 has been a precious promise to me. May it encourage you as well.

The LORD your God in your midst,/ The mighty One will save;/ He will rejoice over you with gladness,/ He will quiet you with His love,/ He will rejoice over you with singing.

About the Author

Jan Frank is a licensed Marriage, Family, and Child Counselor. She has designed and led support groups for sexual abuse survivors for over ten years and has trained professionals, pastors, and lay persons how to minister effectively to them. Her sharing of her own story and the vital issues essential to the healing of survivors, as well as her openness, commitment to the Word of God, and reliance on the Holy Spirit brings hope, comfort, and restoration to hurting people.

Jan Frank is the founder of Free to Care Ministries, a non-profit organization committed to ministering to the needs of individuals and families who have exerienced abuse. She is a frequent speaker at conferences and seminars and has a heart for women who desire a more intimate walk with God.

She and her husband Don conduct seminars nationwide based upon their book *When Victims Marry*, which encourages couples to build a stronger marriage by breaking destructive cycles.

Jan and Don Frank live with their two daughters in Southern California.

You may write to Jan Frank by sending a self-addressed stamped envelope to:

Free to Care Ministries
P.O. Box 1491
Placentia, CA 92670

Notes

Chapter 1

1. Cheryl McCall, "The Cruelest Crime—Sexual Abuse of Children: The Victims, the Offenders, How to Protect Your Family," *Life Magazine* (December 1984), 35.

2. Lois Timnick, "22% in Survey Were Child Abuse Victims," *Los Angeles Times* (August 25, 1985).

Chapter 2

1. David Seamands, *Healing of Memories* (Wheaton, IL: Victor Books, 1985), 79.

2. Seamands, *Memories*, 34.

3. Timnick, "22% in Survey Were Child Abuse Victims."

4. Seamands, *Memories*, 95-96.

5. Roland Summit, "Typical Characteristics of Father-Daughter Incest: A Guide for Investigation" (Unpublished research paper, August 1979).

6. Ellen Weber, "Incest," *Ms.* (April 1977), 38.

Chapter 3

1. Seamands, *Memories*, 38.

Chapter 4

1. Dr. Cecil Osborne, *Understanding Your Past—The Key to Your Future* (Burlingame, CA: Yokefellow Press, 1980), 21, 24.

2. W. H. Missildine, *Your Inner Child of the Past* (New York: Pocket Books, Inc., 1963), 284.

3. Steve and Annie Chapman, "Her Daddy's Love" (Dawn Treader Music, 1983). Used by permission of Gaither Copyright Management. All rights reserved.

Chapter 5

1. James Dobson, *Love Must Be Tough* (Waco, TX: Word, Inc., 1983), 121.

2. D. Kantor and W. Lehr as quoted in *Family Therapy: An Overview*, Irene and Herbert Goldenberg (Monterey, CA: Books/Cole Publishing Co., 1985), 42.

Chapter 6

1 Irene and Herbert Goldenberg, *Family Therapy: An Overview* (Monterey, CA: Brooks/Cole Publishing Co., 1985), 171.

Chapter 7

1. M. A. Lieberman and L. Borman as quoted in *The Theory and Practice of Group Psycho-Therapy*, Irving D. Yalom (New York: Basic Books, Inc., 1985), 106.

2. Charles Swindoll, *Growing Strong in the Seasons of Life* (Portland, OR: Multnomah Press, 1983), 78.

Chapter 8

1. David Augsburger, *Caring Enough to Confront* (Ventura, CA: Regal Books, 1984), 50.

2. Summit, "Typical Characteristics of Father-Daughter Incest."

3. Susan Forward and Craig Buck, *Betrayal of Innocence: Incest and Its Devastation* (New York: Penguin Books, Inc., 1978), 45-46.

4. Myrna Alexander, *Behold Your God: A Woman's Workshop on the Attributes of God* (Grand Rapids, MI: Zondervan Publishing House, n.d.).

Chapter 9

1. Charles Swindoll, *Improving Your Serve* (Waco, TX: Word, Inc., 1981), 61.

2. Seamands, *Memories*, 39.

3. Seamands, *Memories*, 24.

4. Swindoll, *Growing Strong*, 166-67.

5. John Edward Jones with John P. Boneck, *Reconciliation* (Minneapolis: Bethany House Publishers, 1984), 81.

6. Jones and Boneck, *Reconciliation*, 81.

Chapter 10

1. Josh McDowell, *His Image . . . My Image* (San Bernardino, CA: Here's Life Publishers, Inc., 1984), 31.

2. McDowell, *His Image*, 88.

3. William Backus and Marie Chapian, *Telling Yourself the Truth* (Minneapolis: Bethany House Publishers, 1985), 15.

4. Gerald Corey, *Theory and Practice of Counseling and Psychotherapy*, Chapter 11: "Rational-Emotive Therapy" (Monterey, CA: Brooks/Cole Publishing Co., 1982), 175.

5. Lana Bateman, *God's Crippled Children* (self-published book; available through Philippian Ministries, P. O. Box 31122, Dallas, TX 75231).

6. McDowell, *His Image*, 53-54.

7. McDowell, *His Image*, 88.

Commonly Asked Questions about Abuse and Recovery

1. Charles Sell, *Unfinished Business* (Portland, OR: Multnomah, 1989), 42.

Books for Further Reading

Allender, Dr. Dan, *The Wounded Heart*, NavPress

Bateman, Lana, *God's Crippled Children*, (order through Philippian Ministries, 8217 Club Meadows, Dallas, Texas 75243)

Buhler, Rich, *Pain and Pretending*, Thomas Nelson Publishers

Cloud, Henry, and John Townsend, *Boundaries*, Zondervan

Ells, Alfred, *Restoring Innocence*, Thomas Nelson Publishers

Feldmeth, Joanne, and Midge Finley, *We Weep for Ourselves and Our Children*, Harper & Row

Frank, Don and Jan, *When Victims Marry*, Thomas Nelson Publishers

Friesen, Dr. James, *Uncovering the Mystery of MPD*, Here's Life Publishers

Heitritter, Lynn, and Jeanette Vought, *Helping Victims of Sexual Abuse*, Bethany House

Johnson, Karen C., *Through the Tears: Caring for the Sexually Abused Child*, Broadman Press

McClung, Floyd, Jr., *The Father Heart of God*, Harvest House Publishers

Morrison, Jan, *A Safe Place*, Shaw Publishers

Peters, David, *A Betrayal of Innocence*, Word, Inc.

Seamands, David, *Healing for Damaged Emotions*, Victor Books

Seamands, David, *Healing of Memories*, Victor Books

Townsend, Dr. John, *Hiding from Love*, NavPress

Wilson, Sandra, *Released from Shame*, InterVarsity Press